The
Miracle
of
Humble
Leadership

*Helping Good People
Become <u>Great</u>*

by
Hal Chappelear

THE MIRACLE OF HUMBLE LEADERSHIP: HELPING GOOD PEOPLE BECOME GREAT

1405 SW 6th Avenue • Ocala, Florida 34471 • Phone 352-622-1825 • Fax 352-622-1875
Website: www.atlantic-pub.com • Email: sales@atlantic-pub.com
SAN Number: 268-1250

Library of Congress Control Number: 2020922604

Printed in the United States

PROJECT MANAGER: Kassandra White
INTERIOR LAYOUT AND JACKET DESIGN: Nicole Sturk

**TO
BILLIE
MY WIFE
MY FRIEND
MY LOVE**

She loves God, is a devotee of truth, goodness, and beauty,
and is a wellspsring of joy

**DEDICATED TO
THE HONORABLE MEMORY
OF
MALCOLM G. ROGERS**

Ever polite and respectful of others, a model of elegance and grace, a
humble and honorable man worthy of emulation.

Table of Contents

Part III: *The Humble Leader in Action*

Introduction: Why I Wrote the Book

Fresh out of the Medical University of South Carolina with a degree in Pharmacy, I didn't have *leadership* as part of my daily vernacular. As a new, practicing pharmacist, I was oblivious to the role I played as a leader in the drugstore or later in the hospital. It was not until I joined the sales force of The Upjohn Company (now Pfizer, Inc.) and was more immediately impacted by a management structure that it became obvious to me that I would need to be aware of the leadership culture and workplace politics within management if I ever hoped to succeed in a big company. When given my first notable role in leadership, namely district manager, I became responsible for the activity of twelve men who were older in age and more senior in service than myself at age 28. I realized the need to mutually develop effective ways to reach the company's goals that would demonstrate respect for my team's knowledge and experience. It became quite clear early on that the type of management that called for "organizing, directing, and controlling" was not the best way to encourage others to perform a specific task. Furthermore, I learned within that first year how important it was to lead in the interest of these men and build a team made up of trusting, loyal relationships; I also learned that in so doing, my mistakes never made a big splash, because the team's loyalty helped us recover quickly and we all learned from the experience.

Since, like many, I was not given any leadership training, the intensity of this early on-the-job experience forced me to pay attention to what I was doing. As time went on, I became wholeheartedly aware of my inadequacies, and thus devoted myself to becoming a student of literature on leadership and personnel development including: Peter Drucker, who is considered the "founder of modern management"; James McGregor Burns, an authority on leadership studies and known for his contributions to the transactional, transformational, aspirational, and visionary schools of leadership theory; and Douglas McGregor, who is responsible for breaking down previous management styles with X and Y Theory, which created a new role for managers to assume. I studied the lives and leadership style of historical sociopolitical and military leaders: Patton, Yeager, MacArthur, Churchill, Eisenhower, Gandhi, King, etc. As my ability to lead improved and level of responsibility at Upjohn increased, time for personal and professional development for myself and others decreased, and I found it necessary to hire individuals with specific skills to provide counsel, facilitate workshops, lead discussion groups, and perform executive coaching with select individuals. As these well-respected and highly skilled professionals brought many benefits to the company, I personally relished the opportunity to learn from their work as it contributed to my sincere passion for leadership development.

At age 54, I completed 30 years of service to The Upjohn Company. During my final years as Executive Vice President, I was a member of an eleven-person team charged with operating the company and had responsibility for sales, worldwide marketing support, and external affairs. After this extended period with one of the nation's top pharmaceutical companies, I transitioned to one of the nation's top academic institutions, namely the University of Maryland, Baltimore, where I would spend more than 28 years. I worked initially at the School of Pharmacy where, within a few years, we started the pharmaceutical company known as UPM Pharmaceuticals, a division of Gregory Pharmaceutical Holdings, Inc. I performed a variety of duties, which included advisor to the dean and serving as Associate Dean for Entrepreneurism. Over time I transitioned from "employee" to "consultant" and became more engaged in the school's business development activities, strategic planning process, leadership development, and executive coaching for faculty and staff.

After being elected a Member of the Board of Trustees for the University of Maryland Baltimore Foundation, I established relationships with the leadership of all schools across the campus—pharmacy, medicine, social work, graduate studies, dentistry, law, and nursing. By this time, I was well aware of the significant difference in leadership atmospheres between the academic and business communities. Yet, I had found that the people dynamics and development requirements for professionals in all schools were the same.

The newly appointed Dean of the School of Dentistry recognized a difference in ambience between his school and the School of Pharmacy, which the Dean of the Pharmacy School partially credited to the leadership development programs I had been encouraged to facilitate. Thus, I was asked to introduce similar programs in the Dental School and initiate a strategic planning process to more clearly establish a vision for the school and provide action steps that would maintain focus and guide all personnel toward the desired end. During four years of these efforts, there was a Gallup "employee climate survey" conducted at the campus level that focused on a variety of issues, including employee engagement. The results of this survey indicated that employee engagement on campus was the same as that of the American workforce at large, that is to say, 65-70% were classified as disengaged and actively disengaged. The dean recognized the importance of these findings and supported my proposal to initiate a twelve-month trial program designed to impact the well-established, one-hundred-and-eighty-year-old culture, and thus improve the engagement of all employees in the dental school. To that end, we selected 48 members from the faculty and staff, divided them into eight small groups of six people, and initiated an organized program that met once a month for the purpose of establishing close personal and professional relationships. The plan was that these gatherings would lead to a better understanding of their fellow employees, all job requirements, the need to share responsibilities, compliance with the strategic plan, as well as discussion of other major topics that impacted routine activities on the job. We administered Gallup's twelve question survey to all 48 participants at the beginning of the project. After twelve months of the small group discussions, we administered the survey again and realized noteworthy improvement in eleven of the twelve parameters that made up the survey. I also noticed that the leadership's goal of forming closer personal and professional relationships with their colleagues was accomplished and the greater openness and sense of responsibility that re-sulted among the faculty and staff gave the opportunity to negotiate daily challenges with more attention and care. I truly believe it was these indi-viduals' willingness to invest and focus on others and a humble spirit that spread across the groups that gave rise to the commitment to continue the initiative.

I completed my assigned responsibilities at the School of Dentistry in June 2019 and left a method for continuous follow up of the strategic plan and its application, as well as the "small group initiative." I continue to serve the leadership community on campus as a member of the board of trustees for the foundation and executive coach for a few key faculty and staff.

As I reflected on my life experiences and the successful leadership that I witnessed over the years, I came to recognize that the leaders who made the greatest impact in the lives around them, who stimulated the flourishing of others and brought unrivaled success to their institutions, did not be-come who they were via tips and tricks from a management workshop or by adhering to a touted leadership style from a book. Rather, it began with an intentional focus on others and a genuine recognition of their value—a true humility—that was the fuel for a lifetime of admirable leadership. My friend, boss, and mentor, the late Malcolm G. Rogers, epitomized hum-ble leadership. Malcolm was a most influential force to be reckoned with within The Upjohn Company, one you could never describe as milque-toast. He was a very intense and competitive leader and exceedingly ambi-tious for the goals of the company and his team; one of his frequent battle cries was, "No one remembers who came in second!" He also directed his intense focus towards developing a rich understanding of the motivations, personalities, and challenges of those both above and beneath him on the hierarchical ladder. He knew how to show respect and encouragement to each in their own way, endeavored to be their advocate, and only let ed-ifying words pass his lips, no matter the likability or lack thereof of the person in question. He enthusiastically celebrated the success of others and accepted his place in the winner's circle with equal grace. He spearheaded subtle shifts of culture within his circles by speaking with positivity and determination about future changes. Malcolm represented in visible daily form the highest level of integrity and consistently took full responsibility for his behavior. Malcolm was influential in my becoming an Upjohn employee and entering Upjohn's leadership team, and was a personal and professional model that I would attempt to emulate for many years to come.

This book is dedicated to the memory of Malcolm, and his example in my life appears throughout this book. Furthermore, Appendix I is the eulogy I delivered in his memory during his funeral services at the First Presbyterian Church of Florence South Carolina on 30 December 2018.

It is my hope that in my work, you become deeply convinced of the transformative value of a life devoted to others and that you can experience the great rewards of leadership anchored in this very fact. I will share with you my professional challenges and the wisdom I have derived from these challenges and those of others in an attempt to sketch the making of a leader whose daily behavior will yield the joy of success. By focusing on the needs of others, your institution will encourage close-working relationships to emerge where the resulting level of responsibility and respect enables the pursuit and achievement of common goals.

Is Leadership as We Know It Today the Answer to the American Workforce's Challenges?

The world's business, academic, government, religious, and other institutions need responsible men and women to lead them in making positive contributions to the human condition. Our leadership industry has failed to produce these men and women, and it is time to take action.

Major consulting firms report that serious challenges continue to face the world's workforce, despite the efforts of a $366 billion leadership training and development industry.[1] While many factors could be considered contributors to this leadership failure, it seems to be an accurate assessment. Gallup has specifically highlighted that approximately 65-70% of the

---

1. Westfall, Chris. "Leadership Development Is A $366 Billion Industry: Here's Why Most Programs Don't Work." *Forbes*. 20 June 2019.

American workforce is disengaged or actively disengaged in their jobs.[2] If you are wondering how the United States compares to the rest of the world in this regard, the numbers are even more disconcerting, as 87% are labeled as disengaged or actively disengaged, and 26% of those tend to spread their discontent to others. (Data collected from more than 195,600.) Who are the disengaged and actively disengaged employees, and could we recognize them at our workplace? The disengaged employee performs the minimum requirements of the job, is primarily motivated by their paycheck, and finds fulfillment outside of work. While this employee may not cause immediate concern as long as they do their job, there is great tragedy in their untapped potential; if they can become engaged in their place of work, then the individual will surely surprise you and themselves with all that they can bring to the table. The actively disengaged employee dislikes management, their pay, everything about the company and effectively poisons other good employees with their negativity. To be sure, this is a worldwide concern.

On March 15, 2014, an article appeared in *Forbes* titled: "Why Companies Fail To Engage Today's Workforce: The Overwhelmed Employee." Josh Bersin, founder and principal at Bersin by Deloitte, contributed to the article, which began as follows: "We just completed a major study of human capital trends around the world (Deloitte Global Human Capital Trends, 2,500 organizations in 90 countries) and the message is clear: Companies are struggling to engage our modern, 21st-century workforce."[3]

For several years, the Gallup Organization has published the results of their survey of the American workplace.[4] The report for years 2015-2016 was made available in February 2017 and is based on data collected from more than 195,600 U.S. employees via the Gallup Panel and Gallup Daily tracking during that period, and more than 31 million respondents through Gallup's Q[12] Client Database. As one studies the data and reflects on the

2. Gallup Inc. "State of the American Workplace Report," 2017. https://www.gallup.com/workplace/238085/state-american-workplace-report-2017.aspx.

3. Bersin, Josh. "Why Companies Fail to Engage Today's Workforce: The Overwhelmed Employee." *Forbes*. March 15, 2014.

4. Gallup Inc. "State of the American Workplace Report," 2017. https://www.gallup.com/workplace/238085/state-american-workplace-report-2017.aspx.

apparent ineptness of some of today's leadership, redirection of this effort may be in order. For example:

- Twenty percent of employees feel the leader is giving good direction.

- Fifteen percent of employees are inspired about their institution's future.

- Thirteen percent of employees feel confident that their leaders are effectively communicating with the organization.[5]

I encourage you to read the full report. It appears that a new leadership direction is in order.

The report is based on Gallup's in-depth research and was created to help business leaders optimize their attraction, retention, engagement and performance strategies in a time of extraordinary change. The findings speak to best practices, employees' evolving wants and needs, and gives leaders a clear understanding of what it takes to be an exceptional workplace.

Gallup brings more evidence to this claim by highlighting the concerns of leaders:

- 86% of business and HR leaders believe they do not have an adequate leadership pipeline (38% see it as an urgent problem).

- 79% believe they have a significant retention and engagement problem (26% see it as urgent).

- 77% do not feel they have the right HR skills to address the issue (25% urgent).

- 75% are struggling to attract and recruit the top people they need (24% urgent).

---

5. ibid.

- Only 17% feel they have a compelling and engaging employment brand.[6]

Gallup also asked companies "to evaluate their management practices" and found that "they were particularly critical of the way they manage performance, leading us to the conclusion that performance management is broken."

- Only 6% believe their current process for managing performance is worth the time, 58% called their process "weak," with North American companies, 20% worse than the rest of the world.[7]

These statistics all point to the fact that the current "management-focused leadership model" that has dominated workshops, conferences, and literature has not been successful. These programs provide rules and facts that are universally agreed on as good management practices, but are rarely ever implemented. The question is how do we change the model and equip both the "followers" and leaders of the workforce to change the system?

The model of humble leadership that I am proposing gets to the heart of the issue by identifying what motivates and inspires the individual to lead well. True humble leadership requires a genuine focus and passion for the people we lead, without which our leadership skills never make it beyond the workshop. Emboldened by the heart knowledge of why he or she leads, the Humble Leader fosters inspiring, transforming relationships of mutual influence that sustain the growth of individuals, thus institutions. In that pursuit, they recognize that every individual is a leader and thus seek to support and encourage the flourishing of each individual and aim to create a ripple effect through a community, an institution, a culture. Leaders who previously felt they could only encourage the continued development of already successful *engaged* employees will now see that they are uniquely

6. Gallup Inc. "State of the American Workplace Report," 2017. https://www.gallup.com/workplace/238085/state-american-workplace-report-2017.aspx.

7. ibid.

equipped to captivate, champion, and elevate the spirits and abilities of formerly ignored or resented *disengaged* employees. Barbara Kellerman in her book, *Hard Times*, states: "The leadership industry has a problem—a screamingly obvious one. It has failed over its roughly forty-year history to, in any major, meaningful way, improve the human condition."[8] This book will walk you through the challenges that we confront when we seek to be truly "others focused," equip your "better" half to be victorious, and bring to life the virtues, principles, and behaviors that captivate followers of humble leaders.

Our society has unwittingly become engulfed by the maw of self-centeredness. Not only does it characterize our communities and institutions, but the individual is run ragged in search of self-fulfillment and happiness, limiting true human connection to mere collisions with other individuals on the same all too often fruitless search. Leaders cannot be oblivious to the prevalence of narcissistic behavior in our culture's vernacular and thinking, and to this end, any successful leader must firstly be willing to recognize, face, and mitigate these tendencies in themselves. In this book, I seek to convince you of the ineffable and transformative value of focusing on others first, last, and always. This focus is the essence of true humility and the key of successful businesses, enriching institutions, fulfilling communities, and flourishing individuals.

As you join me on this rigorous journey toward developing the most effective form of leadership, I will ask you to answer the questions:

Do you seek to understand and embrace the value of others in all areas of your life and consider it your responsibility to treat them accordingly?

When someone departs your presence, do they leave with joyous inspiration just because they have been in your company?

Do you live your life with a refreshing transparency that encourages others to be genuine?

---

8. Kellerman, Barbara. *Hard Times: Leadership in America.* Stanford Business Books, 2015.

Are you leading yourself and others in such a way that the answer to these questions is a resounding, yes?

Our Journey to Becoming a Humble Leader In Three Parts

In *Part I—A Serious Focus on Humility*, the book delves into an analysis of that which influences our daily decisions: the human soul, mind, and spirit, and exposes the consistent prevalence of narcissistic behavior rooted in pride within each of us. This study of unadmitted, self-focused tendencies is of critical importance if we are to pursue lasting change within ourselves and become equipped to encourage the flourishing of others. Next, the section introduces the true worth and power of humility, as it is a virtue all too often belied by false pretenders—those who see humility as another achievement to flaunt. With this dichotomy of tendencies in mind, the section stresses the importance of recognizing the power in our choices to create and develop highly regarded institutions that are made up of inspired individuals. Furthermore, the author encourages us all to pay greater attention to the responsibility we have to ourselves and others in our daily lives.

Part II: Core Virtues of the Humble Leader presents us with the prism through which we see the core virtues of the Humble Leader. Social media reflects a thin veneer of what we wish others to see in us. However, the still water of a humble leader runs much deeper, and it is often that portion of the glacier below the surface—the practiced virtues of these men and women—that truly captivates and attracts others to them. These ageless virtues might be widely recognized, but because they have been severely undervalued and often distorted, they are not commonplace. The author interviewed and spoke at length with various institutional leaders such as those associated with national health organizations, the financial community, pharmaceutical industry, in addition to others who hold prominent positions in other areas such as the Chancellor of the University System of Maryland, Superintendent of United States Naval Academy, President of the Medical University of South Carolina, and President of Clemson University. In these conversations, it became clear that certain core virtues characterized these individuals and undergirded their success throughout their personal and professional journeys. It is in this light that these core virtues are presented, as fuel necessary to the development of humble leaders. The author encourages his readers to continuously meditate on these values throughout the book, because he is convinced the practice of these virtues promises transformative power within ourselves and in our relationships with others.

Part III: The Humble Leader in Action discusses the fact that we are relational beings, and when we plant ourselves in the soil of this truth, we become active, thriving, and responsible parts of the community and integral to its culture. Humble leaders intentionally bring the previously discussed core virtues from their subconscious to the forefront of their minds, and as a result, they assume a greater level of prominence in their communities and their very behavior provides the impetus for new values to flourish in the culture as others seek to follow their lead. In light of this, leaders are shown to be responsible for their daily behavior within and without the workplace, and thus, we explore what kind of action is in concert with, promotes, and is the fruit of these values and virtues. Leaders can be the instrument of necessary change when they thoughtfully consider and employ these virtues in their daily activities: how they communicate with others, how they deal with negotiations and manage conflict, and how they develop and empower others. Such thoughtful and intentional behavior is incredibly powerful and as such quite difficult to maintain. The author employs scientific proof to gird his readers' confidence that this change is holistic and achievable, and he provides tangible tools for forming new habits. Key to this transformation is the identification and establishment of a clearly defined purpose that answers the questions: "Why do I go to work each day?", "Why do others matter?", "Why do I maintain a positive perspective?". Purpose is the fertile soil that infuses life into the idea of miracles.

The humble leader is worthy of emulation and among the most exalted personage within society. However, rather than being marveled over for how they have obtained such high status, esteem, fame or fortune, their behavior clearly attests to their appeal as central figures in the creation and growth of major institutions and respected members of the "ordinary" community. The way they conduct themselves in formal or informal settings encourages others to become engaged whether at work or play.

When you finish reading his book, you will have a broad understanding of humble leadership, the unique challenges that the humble leader faces each day and the high level of corporate gratitude and job satisfaction that follows a job well done. In addition to personal experience and that which is available in published literature, you will have information that came from extensive conversations and formal interviews with leaders of major institutions. Finally, you will have a variety of "must dos" as you begin or continue walking your developmental path to humble leadership and experience the joys of accomplishment as these "must dos" become common to your behavior and associated with personal and professional success.

PART I

A Serious Focus on Humility

CHAPTER 1: The Disengaged Employee:
Is Pride the Roadblock?

A major problem faced by leadership within any institution or community is the disengagement of those they lead. The Gallup Organization has made it quite clear that as of December 2016 only one third of the American workforce is engaged in their jobs. As stated by Jim Clifton, Chairman and CEO of Gallup:

> The American workforce has more than 100 million full-time employees. One-third of those employees are what Gallup calls engaged at work. They love their jobs and make their organization and America better every day. At the other end, 16% of employees are actively disengaged—they are miserable in the workplace and destroy what the most engaged employees build. The remaining 51% of employees are not engaged—they're just there.[9]

Deloitte and Touche attempted to identify the core problem inherent in the system: "Today employees don't want a career; they want an experience."[10] Most of us will spend the majority of our productive years on the job, and understandably desire our efforts to contribute to a worthwhile positive experience, rather than constantly feeling overwhelmed and over-

---

9. Clifton, Jim. "State of the American Workplace Report." Workplace Disruption: From Annual Reviews to Coaching." Gallup Workplace, *Gallup*, 15 Feb. 2017. *https://www.gallup.com/workplace/238085/state-american-workplace-report-2017.aspx.*

10. Bersin, Josh. "Why Companies Fail to Engage Today's Workforce—the Overwhelmed Employee." *Forbes*, March 15, 2015. https://www.forbes.com/sites/joshbersin/2014/03/15/why-companies-fail-to-engage-todays-workforce-the-overwhelmed-employee/#37f27cc44726.

worked, without any hope of a healthy work-life balance. However, there are those, both in management and the workforce, who are content with the current management-focused leadership model and point to the success of the American economy as evidence that disengagement should not concern us. The desire for a workplace experience that is satisfying and engaging should not be so quickly dismissed, as there is a great tragedy in the ignored, untapped potential in this majority of the workforce. Imagine if leadership were equipped to not only halt the destructive tendencies of the actively disengaged, but to captivate and inspire the half of the workforce to go above and beyond minimum job requirements. Across high-ranking institutions leadership has rarely had this vision, let alone been equipped to pursue employee engagement. Furthermore, this leadership model creates artificial distinctions between leaders and followers that ignore the basic fact that each of us has a sphere of influence who we daily lead through our actions. In actuality, regardless of the formal title we bear, we must oscillate from leading and following many times throughout a single day to be successful. The self-centered focus of our culture has sustained the current leadership model, which too often caters to a "What's in it for me?" attitude through "organization, direction, and control" of employees. From my experience of observing the workforce in a variety of settings over the years—government, business, academic, religious, non-profits—I would say that this paradigm is standard operating procedure for most of us.

Since the Second World War we have been slowly and decisively transforming our society to one dominated by hyphenated words: self-image, self-esteem, self-assertion, self-determination. As we have done so, we have slowly removed the absoluteness of moral law, supremacy of love, and the salt of extraordinary purity. It seems that the order of the day is relevance, where, in the interest of appropriate behavior, one decides for him or herself what is right or wrong, good or bad, or even true or false. There are those who claim we live in a *post-truth* society, one in which objective facts are less influential in shaping public opinion than appeals to emotion and personal belief (post-truth was even the Oxford English Dictionary's word of the year for 2016). Our culture steeps us in suspicion and doubt, and we meet all authority with questions.

Many people have attempted to address this issue. For example, David Brooks wrote in his recent book, *The Second Mountain:*

> For six decades the worship of the self has been the central occupation of our culture—molding the self, investing in the self, expressing the self. Capitalism, the meritocracy, and modern social science have normalized selfishness; they have made it seem that the only human motives that are real are the self-interested ones—the desire for money, status, and power.[11]

Under this assessment of our current society, it is no wonder that many of our institutions' top leaders and followers are intellectually crippled by a culture that has normalized selfishness and are blind to its impact on employee engagement. In this initial chapter, we believe it is critical to make a study of the individual worker and this narcissistic parasite within each of us if we are to truly recognize the challenging task before us. In the following pages, I will present research and arguments from top neuroscientists, psychologists, classical literature, and modern media to help us understand the selfish epidemic plaguing our institutions and communities.

Firstly, we need to understand the meaning of narcissism and the prevalence of its widespread existence.

Peter Gray, Ph.D.,[12] research professor at Boston College, posted an article in *Psychology Today* titled, "Why Is Narcissism Increasing Among Young Americans?" In this document he discusses the serious social and psychological problem associated with this condition, and his writing brings to mind the unrest we currently—spring and summer 2020—see in many of our major cities. It appears that the young people participating in this disruptive behavior are self-centered and demonstrate an air of superiority. They are angry at people in general for a variety of reasons, not the least of which is the community's failure to recognize them as "superior" beings.

---

11. Brooks, David. *The Second Mountain: How People Move from the Prison of Self to the Joy of Commitment.* Penguin Random House, 2019.

12. Gray, Peter. Web log. *Why Is Narcissism Increasing among Young Americans* (blog), January 16, 2014. psychologytoday.com.

They are unhappy, exhibit a sense of entitlement, and apparently are not constrained by the laws of the land. Without belaboring the point, let's accept the facts that narcissism is bad for the community and is bad for the individual. A narcissist has difficulty forming deep, meaningful relationships and is living a life in complete contradiction to that of a humble leader.

Each of us exhibit narcissistic behavior at one time or another; I dare say daily. Narcissism will deter our ability to be effective leaders of our institutions and engaging members of our communities by hindering us from establishing relationships and sharing beliefs winsomely. It is important to recognize how integral narcissistic tendencies are to our nature and limit its prevalence within our daily behavior.

One such example of this phenomena, which will undoubtedly be relatable, was easily recognized at the many receptions at Upjohn, one of our nation's top pharmaceutical companies, where I held my first leadership position. These receptions occurred before meetings, in between meetings, after meetings, and if the meeting was too boring, while the meeting was under way! There was a mid-high-level executive at Upjohn—I will give him the name Carl—who was referred to by his peer group as "Butterfly." He was given this name because during any reception, Carl would enter the room, immediately seek the highest-ranking person, and "corral" that person until the next, higher or more influential person appeared. Carl was so inclined toward his own self-interest that he would make every effort to capture the attention of the "boss." To that end, he would leave his current "prisoner" in mid-conversation if the next incoming person was of enough rank or importance. While this behavior was somewhat rare among other employees, he developed it to an "art form." Over the years, he became so well known for these actions that his colleagues tended to ignore him on important business issues. While he was a good employee otherwise and had a great deal to offer, Carl lost his ability to be a part of the serious business community, his relationships suffered, his credibility became questionable, and in the end, he was viewed as a lightweight whose interest were so self-serving that his value as a "business colleague" was essentially de minimis. He retired early. I wonder what the outcome would have been if instead of merely trying to advance his own career, Carl broached conversation with these higher ranking individuals with the goal of gathering information about company happenings or learning skills to help his colleagues or to truly better the company. Or what if Carl used his skills as the "social butterfly" to help others gain a voice in discussion with top leaders?

When I speak of narcissistic behavior, it should be noted that narcissism as a "personality disorder" is not very prevalent. According to the Diagnostic and Statistical Manual of Mental Disorders, between 0.5 and 1.0% of the general population is diagnosed with this condition.[13] However, the fact that very few of us could actually be diagnosed with the personality disorder narcissism should not give us comfort; narcissistic behavior or tendencies are easily recognized across our institutions. Those who have spent time with children will recognize that we all begin to exhibit narcissistic behavior at a very young age, and as we get older, this "childhood narcissism" matures within our individualistic, self-sufficient society into what we may more readily identify as "adult pride." One antidote to this phenomena is to guard against the development of pride or over exaggerated self–confidence, to allow healthy critique of the embellished story we tell about ourselves, to fight the tendency to "see myself as bigger than life." In Chapter 6 of Dr. Jordan Peterson's book *Twelve Rules for Life: An Antidote for Chaos*, he emphasizes over and over again: "clean up your own house before you try cleaning up mine."[14] Or in other language, before you are compelled to redirect another, redirect yourself. Each of us has a tendency towards the "my way or the highway" attitude. But before you send someone to said highway, have you checked to see if it is clean and straightforward? The all too common "don't do as I do but as I say" ideology puts before our employees the unnecessary burden of overcoming our negative baggage in order to see the way forward. It is incumbent upon each of us to accept the responsibility to lead ourselves as well as others. In keeping with the thoughts of John Maxwell, a well-known author, speaker,

---

13. American Psychiatric Association, *Diagnostic and Statistical Manual of Mental Disorders*, Fifth Edition. Arlington, VA: American Psychiatric Association, 2013.

14. Peterson, Jordan B., et al. *12 Rules for Life: an Antidote to Chaos*. Random House Canada, 2019.

leadership guru and pastor, "We as leaders are to know the way, go the way and show the way."[15]

How far does pride reign in our day-to-day lives? Jonathan Edwards, a Protestant minister, philosopher, and theologian, elucidates the nature and effects of pride, specifically in relation to spiritual matters—what one may term "religiosity"—in his book, *Thoughts on New England Revival*.[16] Below I reflect on three effects of pride discussed by Edwards in comparison with humility:

1. Pride leads you to have an air of contempt and disdain.

With some exceptions, a marriage or any other relationship can survive almost any challenge except that of contempt; when one partner considers the other unworthy or inferior and deigns not to be in the presence of that person, a way forward becomes nearly impossible. In contrast, the humble person may well recognize faults in others but considers them with optimism and understanding. The tendency of the humble person is to build on another's strengths in an effort to minimize the impact of weaknesses.

2. Pride makes us quick to criticize others and then shun those whom we have criticized or who have criticized us.

This critical attitude is a particularly poisonous effect of prideful behavior. If we fail to make an effort to see better in others, pride only illuminates another's faults, even though those same faults may well exist in us. When we criticize others, they can often feel socially inept or personally unappealing, and they will avoid social interaction for fear of being ridiculed, humiliated, rejected or disliked. In contrast, the humble person is disposed to be far more aware of his or her own faults than others and is inclined to find the good in others. The humble person is disinclined to criticize,

15. Maxwell, John. "John C. Maxwell Quotes," Brainy Quote. https://www.brainyquote.com/quotes/john_c_maxwell_383606.

16. Edwards, Jonathan. *Thoughts on the New England Revival*. Carlisle, PA: Banner of Truth, 2005. (original publishing date was 1742).

seeks understanding of differences, and is loyal through difficult times—the humble person doesn't give up.

3. A proud person is dogmatic and sure about every point of their beliefs.

This person never has a single doubt! Moreover, proud people cannot distinguish between major and minor points of belief because everything is major. The humble person is open to different points of view, since they respect and value the input from others and accepts doubt as a stimulant to thoughtful consideration and discourse. Author Dallas Willard once said it well: "If you're going to be a doubter, you need to believe your beliefs and doubt your doubts, as well as to doubt your beliefs and believe your doubts."[17] This is how knowledge grows. The humble person encourages others to admit and talk about their doubts, as well as their beliefs.

In Edwards' book, he spoke of a "revival," which referred to a revitalization of religious fervor or church traditions. Edwards argued that this fervor dies due to infighting caused by spiritual pride—the viper that kills community. Pride and its hatchling narcissism is a default setting, integral to the human condition. We are selfish and self-centered. We seek comfort—mental, emotional, personal, professional, and more. Furthermore, we often seek recognition by engaging in competitive opportunities where we have an opportunity to "win" and take pride in our own accomplishments. There is however an opposite side to human nature, which too often lies dormant: the potential for good. The choices we make determine which potency prevails and consequently which side is nourished.

The well-known novella, *Strange Case of Dr. Jekyll and Mr. Hyde,* written by the Scottish author Robert Louis Stevenson centers upon a conception of humanity as dual in nature: both good and evil. Dr. Jekyll conducted experiments in an attempt to separate the two sides of human nature and destroy the evil one. Dr. Jekyll and Mr. Hyde is an examination of this

---

17. Willard, Dallas. *The Allure of Gentleness: Defending the Faith in the Manner of Jesus.* Harper One, 2015.

duality in human nature, as most clearly expressed in the revelation that Mr. Hyde is, in fact, Dr. Jekyll, only transformed into a personification of Jekyll's evil characteristics. The doctor discovered that the evil part of his nature was in some sense natural and part of the whole. Because we cannot perform the same experiment as Dr. Jekyll, the story forces us to confront the fact that these basic elements cannot truly be separated, and furthermore that man is defined by the conflict within his inner nature and how he deals with this duality.

Do you disagree with Mr. Stevenson and reject the notion that mankind has an inherent dark side? This was also the position of Martha Beatrice Webb (1858—1943), an English sociologist and economist, and the woman who coined the phrase "collective bargaining." She was considered by many to have been a major player in developing Britain's modern welfare state. Dr. Tim Keller in his book *Counterfeit Gods* quoted her as follows:

> Somewhere in my diary—1890?—I wrote "I have staked all on the essential goodness of human nature..." [Now thirty-five years later I realize] how permanent are the evil impulses and instincts in man—how little you can count on changing some of these—for instance the appeal of wealth and power—by change in the [social] machinery... No amount of knowledge or science will be of any avail unless we can curb the bad impulse.[18]

Dr. Keller, as others of his ilk, has spoken and written extensively on the counterfeit idols in our society, two of which are power and money. Ms. Webb, seriously interested in advancing the principles of democratic socialism, considered these to be "evil gods" of man and a roadblock to her efforts to promote greater equality of power, wealth and opportunity.

The human heart has not improved in the 21st century. *Aeon*, a digital magazine, published an article in 2018 entitled, "The bad news on human nature, in 10 findings from psychology." This article, published in asso-

---

18. Keller, Tim. *Counterfeit Gods: The Empty Promises of Money, Sex, and Power, and the Only Hope That Matters.* Dutton, 2009.

ciation with *the British Psychological Society's Research Digest*, was written by Christian Jarrett, a cognitive neuroscientist turned science writer and editor of *BPS Research Digest*.

Dr. Jarrett suggests that we have been asking over the years whether humans are *good*, i.e., they show compassion, behave in the interest of others, accept others' needs and desires to be of paramount importance and place them above their own, or *evil*, i.e., they are wicked, immoral, and self-centered, tending to look out for themselves first and often at the expense of others. Even though there no easy answers, humans differ, and we find evidence of the brighter—good—side, as well as the darker—evil—side of human nature. According to his research, the darker side of humanity finds that:

1. People who are culturally, ethnically, or racially different from us are subordinate to us, even less than human.

2. We take pleasure on another person's distress.

3. The oppressed deserve their lot in life.

4. We are insistent, vain, overconfident, and moral hypocrites.

5. We often say inappropriate things to get a rise out of others.

6. We migrate toward deranged, often ineffective leaders.

Jarrett closed the article by stating that "we shouldn't get too down," because "these findings say nothing of the success that some of us have had in overcoming our baser instincts. In fact, it is arguably by acknowledging and understanding our shortcomings that we can more successfully overcome them, and so cultivate the better angels of our nature."[19]

Those of us who have a Judeo-Christian religious orientation should be familiar with the notion of mankind's own dual nature. According to the Scriptures, man was created perfect, in the image of God, and given a free will—the wherewithal to choose between good and evil. St. Augustine of Hippo taught that Adam chose evil. This resulted in the eternal death of

---

19. ibid.

humanity, leaving us with an impaired, though not destroyed, freedom of will. In *Paradise Lost,* Milton[20] describes this corruption of the will and our understanding through the words of Adam to Eve, after they have bitten of the fruit of the knowledge of good and evil:

> Oh Eve, in evil hour thou didst give ear
> To that false worm, of whomsoever taught
> To counterfeit Man's voice; true in our fall,
> False in our promised rising; since our eyes
> Opened we find indeed, and find we know
> Both good and evil; good lost, and evil got;
> Bad fruit of knowledge, if this be to know;
> Which leaves us naked thus, of honor void,
> Of innocence, of faith, of purity,
> Our wonted ornaments now soiled and stained
> And in our faces evident the signs
> Of foul concupiscence; when evil store;
> Even shame, the last of evils; of the first
> Be sure then. How shall I behold the face
> Henceforth of God or angel, erst with joy
> And rapture so oft beheld?

Milton expresses through the words of Adam here that humankind corrupted its good nature when it received the knowledge of good and evil; evil consumed and darkened Adam and Eve's vision and comprehension of what is good. The Apostle Paul elaborates on this dualism in human nature, which he terms the spiritual and physical. The physical being represents our inherent "evil" desires, while its opposite—the spirit—represents our "good" desires. In his writings to the Romans, we read: "For I know that nothing good dwells in me, that is, in my flesh; for the willing is present in me, but the doing of the good is not."[21] In his writing to the Galatians, we read: "For the flesh sets its desire against the Spirit, and the Spirit against

---

20. Milton, John. "Book IX," *Paradise Lost,* New York, Random House, 2008. Lines: 1067-1082.
21. Rom. 7:18, NLT.

the flesh; for these are in opposition to one another…"[22] This is as true today as it was many years ago, yet the thought may make one wonder how deeply our inherently evil tendencies affect our daily choices. After all, there's a big difference between our own selfish tendencies and those who commit atrocities.

A few years ago, there was a plan to produce a miniseries about Hitler's early life. As soon as the word got out that this series was "in the making," criticism emerged from all corners. I read an article in *The New York Times* by Bernard Weinraub, "Planned Mini-Series on Hitler's Early Life Brings Criticism," and it appears that the project's critics felt a mandate to express their opinion, even though they had not read the script. While no one can defend his horrific actions as an adult, the curious may wonder what he was like as a child and what was there about this individual that gave rise to the awful, horrifying individual we know about today. It appears their knowledge of Hitler's older years gave the impression that he was the same during his younger years, and, as stated by Abraham H. Foxman, the national director of the Anti-Defamation League, "Why the need or desire to make this monster a human?" The impression I got from reading the article was that a miniseries would inadvertently create feelings of sorrow or pity for an evil someone who willfully orchestrated the taking of millions of lives.

In September 2002, the movie *Max* was released at the Toronto Film Festival. In December 2002, Jamie Malanowski[23] wrote the article, "Human, Yes, But No Less A Monster," which appeared in the N. Y. Times. Here are a few comments based on the article, as well as thoughts shared by Merino Meyjes, the Dutch writer and director of *Max*.

The director said he read books by Albert Speer, a close ally of Hitler and Minister of Armaments and War Production in Nazi Germany, and Ron Rosenbaum, an American literary journalist that pointed him to the idea

---

22. Gal. 5:17, NLT.

23. Malanowski, Jamie. "Human, Yes, But No Less A Monster." *The New York Times,* December 22, 2002, Section 2, Page 1.

that Hitler was a socially unconventional individual who was closely associated with the arts and a person living in Austria, sporting long hair just
like anyone else's hair.

Meyjes reached the opinion that even though he had always seen Hitler
as a deranged, unstable, and horrible man, he was not born that way. His
attempt to become an artist didn't work out, and he found that a choice
focused on evil was much easier. In the end, Meyer thought the movie
worthwhile and asked himself if he had the nerve to make it.

As I understand it, the movie isn't about Hitler's great crimes because they
are already well known. The movie is about Hitler's small crimes, his emotional cowardice, his relentless self-pity, his envy of others, his frustration,
the way he collected and nurtured offenses, and his desperate need for
recognition. To be sure, the later part of Hitler's life is a near perfect representation of an uncomplicated picture of evil. We can reflect on what we
know and say, "Look at how atrocious he was!" while adding that we could
never do anything like that! But as we read about his life, we realize that
nobody wakes up one day and slaughters thousands.

The point of sharing this story is to emphasize the absolute need to choose
good. Hitler chose to be an artist and failed. Rather than choosing another
path, a path at which he may have been successful, he turned to the default
choice, evil, and an untold number of lives were sacrificed in the end. We
make choices, one at a time. This may shock you but there is the potential in each of us to become like Hitler. It can begin with not forgiving
somebody and nursing a grudge. Imagine someone has wronged you, humiliated you. Your natural need for recognition has been wounded deeply.
Instead of repenting of your pride, instead of forgiving the person who
may have really wronged you, you nurse the grudge. It is always easier to
keep the grudge, to keep your frustration, to nurture your self-pity than to
forgive. Now any relation or friend of the person who wronged you, maybe
even someone who just reminds you in some small way of your persecutor,
also triggers your contempt and resentment. Every time you take the easier
choice, the selfish choice, you move yourself toward becoming more like

the person you don't want to become! To be sure, many small choices eventually make the big ones easier.

This book is not a commentary on Jekyll and Hyde, the opinions of a sociologist or a neuroscientist, Adam and Eve, Paul's writings, or a Hitler movie. My only desire is to prompt sincere self-reflection, inspired by a wide variety of authorities on human nature. If it is our aim to reduce, rather than add to, the growing numbers of disengaged employees who currently represent the majority, then I believe we must seize pride's antidote and pursue humble leadership daily. In order to understand the richness that true humility offers us, let alone the task of humble leadership, we must intimately understand the battle we as leaders and those who follow us must wage against pride. It is imperative that we take personal responsibility for our own emotions and motivations and maintain focus on the value of others. As we recognize our responsibility to others and begin to hush the voice of pride within us, all desired elements of growth will accrue. This daily choice gives us the underappreciated gift of being able to recognize the inherent value of the human lives around us. Furthermore, the humble leader will see that his actions of humble giving inspire the same spirit in others and brings a greater return than he could have ever achieved on his own; it simply requires a step of faith.

It is my conviction that whether we fight to foster a spirit of humility in ourselves and those we lead or succumb to the easier impulse of pride, the potency that we nourish is the one that will dominate in any given setting. As we all know, the vast majority of our decisions are emotional in nature. My intent with this book is to make us aware of the nobler, albeit more difficult path and provide nourishment for the humility sewn within each of us—a seed of greatness—so that it may grow into a more dominant and sincere tendency. We are capable of doing great good as well as causing great harm. This capability is a choice, and it is important to recognize that emotional intelligence—understanding and managing our own emotions, as well as understanding and influencing the emotions of others—contributes to the development of strengths and reduction of weaknesses.

APPLICATION QUESTIONS

- Have I seen Edwards' five effects of pride in others? Have I seen it happen in myself?

- When and how often do I exhibit narcissistic tendencies? Pay attention and make note of your habits for a week.

- Have you ever known a humble leader? What are notable elements of their behavior?

- What must you do in your workplace to offer your colleagues a career, as well as a work experience?

- How may you introduce and maintain a discussion about making good choices?

CHAPTER 2: Pursuit of Employee Engagement: *Humility, the Way Forward*

After our journey within the last chapter exploring the darker side of human behavior, I now believe it is incumbent upon us to give focus to the miraculous potential of humble leadership that is alluded to in the title of this work. I will comment frequently on the seeds of greatness that exist within each of us. Every person is fertile soil for the realization of all the good and desirable things of this life, but these seeds can only germinate to their fullest if they are fed with sincere humility.

First, we must address the elephant in the room. What images are brought to your mind when I speak of humility? Do you see someone who is timid, someone with a weak, self-deprecating character who never speaks up for himself or herself? In the next few paragraphs, I will share my own view of what true humility is, which is defined by the life I have lived and the experiences of other worthy leaders. I will then provide several strategies for self-assessment according to this trait, and I will ask you as my reader to reflect on your own life journey and decide what view of humility will motivate, direct, and empower you to take responsibility for yourself and others.

Humility may be best understood by seeing its role within four key arenas of the human experience. The first is self-worth; it is the answer to the question "Who am I and what value do I place on myself?" The next is my personal relationships with another—I must ask, "Do I have a positive, productive attitude about forming and maintaining relationships?" Next, I must assess how I develop those relationship skills that impact our communities at large and ask, "What are my goals when I socialize? Do I find it useful or important to be a member of a community and why?" Lastly, I must deeply appreciate the breadth and depth of the world, the ideas of those who inhabit it, and this realization must inform how tightly I cling to my own ideas and encourage me to prioritize pursuit of the good, the true and the beautiful above my own pride. In other words, if I, emotionally, never leave home, everything continues to look like home and I must ask, "Can I truly and effectively establish a malleable and life-giving perspective that reflects the appropriate respect for others?"

Now as we continue to explore each of these four components of humility; please meditate on your own answers to the questions below.

1. "Who am I, and what value do I place on myself?"

One may say, "I am whomever I want to be, and my value is determined by myself." As mentioned above, we know that within us are those seeds of greatness. The degree to which the seeds are developed and the course we follow for their development can in fact be controlled by us. All influences in our lives will affect the outcome of this effort; with certain fertilizers our seeds of greatness can grow into the bane of the community, while other fertilizers can mature our seeds into the joy or delight of our communities. It is important that we make the right choice when it comes to the nutrition of our hearts and minds. We must use discernment with the influences in our lives—what is the fruit behind the words of the people we speak to, the books we read, the movies we watch and so forth? Furthermore, as we assess our identity, attempt to identify and further establish personal value, is our focus on ourselves or do we have others in mind? Do we develop the wherewithal to selfishly light our own path or do we want our light to become the beacon that lights the path for others?

Here I would like to proffer some insight into my own answer to this question, as it is inextricably tied to my faith and the fact that I am a child of the Most High God. As His child, I am made in

His image. I am created and equipped to bring unique value to the world He has created and have the responsibility to serve others with my God given gifts.

2. "Do I have a positive, productive attitude about forming and maintaining relationships?"

If we want to reap a life of personal integrity and purpose, we must cultivate relationships that will challenge and encourage us. These relationships must be mutually influential, transformative, and inspirational, and stem from a sincere respect for each other. Every leader needs to develop a few close friendships with people who share common core values and goals and will lovingly hold each other responsible for maintaining those core values while in pursuit of these goals. It is thus that such a relationship inspires each member to continually reach higher levels of motivation, morality, and the fulfillment of their purpose.

3. "What are my goals when I socialize? Do I find it useful or important to be a member of community, and why?"

Community is meant to deeply influence and mold each of its members to such a degree that the absence of one of its members changes not only the whole but each individual part; that is to say: One person brings out characteristics of another that are not brought out in the absence of that person. This is a picture of a community that is most closely connected and continually evolving. The realm of one's impact is not limited to those one is in immediate contact with. Our communities extend our influence, and therefore our responsibility to humankind. If you do the math, it is possible to know as many as a million people throughout our lifetime, and thus, it is reasonable to assume that as a part of our communities, we will influence many millions before we die. We are not simply "who we intend to be" but are products of our family and our culture... a product of our primary community. Community influences our personal development and gives us the ability to influence the development of others. The transformative value of community must not be diminished.

4. "Can I truly and effectively establish an adaptable and life-giving perspective that reflects the appropriate respect for others?"

Perspective, in this case, relies on our own thinking and understanding. We must admit that we choose a "perspective," and the resultant is an associated belief. The question is what part of *us* drives our choice—is it our pride or the desire to be proven right or the most cultured? A wise perspective calls us to learn both sides or several different aspects of an issue. Rather than focus on our own "hometown" point of view, it calls us to seek a common vision and shared goals. It calls us to remember, and most of all, to reflect on how much we allow our experiences of the world beyond us to affect those activities. To be sure, if we take a step of faith and choose to seek out what is true, good, and beautiful, we will surely find it in every culture, nation, and individual. These discoveries will not bring us shame, as our pride might fear, but rather delight, wisdom, and reverence for the world and its inhabitants.

As you ponder the role of humility in these key aspects of your life, you may be asking, "Am I humble?" A few years ago, I had the privilege of listening to a discussion facilitated by Colonel Arthur J. Athens, United States Marine Core, now retired.[24] Col. Athens' entire discussion focused on humility as the key element in leadership. Col. Athens has developed a "humility" survey that focuses on fourteen behaviors, which the participant can give one of three ratings: *I almost never exhibit this behavior; I occasionally exhibit this behavior; I frequently exhibit this behavior.* He claims no statistical significance for the self-administered survey, but for his personal interest, he completes the survey from time to time from his point of view and asks his wife to do the same. After completion, they discuss his

---

24. From 2007-2018, Colonel Athens was the Director of the U.S. Naval Academy's Vice Admiral James B. Stockdale Center for Ethical Leadership and a member of the Academy's Senior Leadership Team.

view of himself in comparison to his wife's view of him. The following is his humility survey:

1. Am I resistant to receiving help from others?

2. Do I have unresolved conflicts with others?

3. Am I reluctant to tell others when they're wrong?

4. Am I offended when others correct me?

5. Am I unwilling to yield to others, even with the minor issues?

6. Am I upset when not recognized for personal achievements?

7. Am I jealous when peers are successful?

8. Do others consider me standoffish?

9. Am I self-conscious in public, overly concerned about what others think?

10. Do I remain stoic when overwhelmed by either sorrow or joy?

11. Is my circle of friends made up of very similar people—same color, same ethnicity, same socio-economic background?

12. Do I have material possessions just to impress others?

13. Do I not particularly pay attention to the handicapped, the elderly, and small children?

14. Do I have trouble remembering others' names?

As the discussion came to an end, Col. Athens stated: "There is no checklist where, on it, you can check off 'humility' and be done with it. Humility is a daily decision and a lifetime commitment. The higher we go, the deeper our foundation of humility needs to be, but it is worth the battle." Additionally, he shared: "I try to start every day with a reminder: This isn't about me. It's about mission, people, and service. Find your reminder. And find role models who live and lead this way. People you can look up to and say, 'That's what it looks like.'"

What were your thoughts as you read through the survey? Do you struggle daily and fall short, *as I do*, to be humble? Furthermore, do you wish you were more humble? I did not include this survey as a tool to shame you, but rather to reveal how we must all struggle to be humble every day—it is not a natural mode of being. However, even if it does not come naturally to us to be humble, I believe humankind's capacity to flourish is intrinsically dependent on our pursuit of humble leadership. I know—that's a big claim, but first let me describe what I mean by flourishing and then, perhaps the connection will become clear.

Human existence is composed of an individual's characteristics and key life events, such as birth, growth, emotionality, aspiration, conflict, and mortality. After surveying a wide range of definitions, I view the term as a vigorous mental and physical state of the individual who is resilient, productive, and enjoys the emergence of each day and the opportunity to thrive and become just a little better than he or she was the day before. It should be made clear that flourishing includes a focus on the most advantageous life for yourself, family, and others and the inspiration to continue growth, irrespective of the day's events. The flourishing individual communicates to others the value of a positive life and the importance of all that is good. This may come across as a "dry" collection of well-chosen words, correctly placed in sentences that give us a fairly well-accepted definition of the concept, human flourishing. What do you think flourishing means to the life we try to live each day?

I believe everything I think, say or do, whether it's positive, negative, or somewhere in between, does impact the flourishing of my life and that of others.

It should be kept in mind that flourishing includes our response (and those whom we lead) to all aspects of life including that which is tragic, disappointing, and painful. The number of ways we can be hurt can be quite long but remember that life must go on! A good leader must prepare his followers for the full spectrum of life. Tim Keller, in his book *Walking with God through Pain and Suffering,* aptly quotes one of his favorite authors, Ernest Becker, on this very subject: "I think that taking life seriously means something like this: that whatever man does on this planet has to be done in the lived truth of the terror of creation… of the rumble of panic underneath everything. Otherwise it is false."[25] In one of Keller's sermons, he also refers to a great line from Macbeth that goes like this:

Each morn new
New widows howl, new orphans cry, and new sorrows
Strike heaven on the face, that it resounds
As if it felt with Scotland and yelled out
Like syllable of dolor.[26]

And to make his point, he continues with a story in which he states, "Kathy and I spent last weekend with one of our best friends whose husband, also one of our best friends, died a month ago. She described to us what it was like to wake up the first morning after her husband died." No doubt you could imagine how you would feel after having experienced such a tragedy.

I haven't experienced many of these tragic events but know people who have experienced all of them and more. Also, while I have "skated by" thus far, it is likely something will come my way in the future. What must I do now and in the future in order to flourish in all possible circumstances? What would you say to the friend whose husband just died?

You and I could continue to identify the complex issues we must deal with each day; death, illness, or other negative experiences speak to the complexity of life. A truly humble individual, who is always there when one needs them, and who is driven by sincere empathy, dare I say love for another, will share all their resources and go to whatever lengths to be an aid to their friend in pain; in this way, humility can be the antidote to the impact of these harmful elements that exist to do us harm.

To be the person that I described in the last sentence, you may be asking what will be required of you. Empathy is not enough. Caring is not enough.

---

25. Keller, Timothy. *Walking with God through Pain and Suffering.* Penguin Books, 2016.
26. Shakespeare, William. *Macbeth.* Folger Shakespeare Library. Act 4. Scene 3, lines 4-7.

But as mentioned earlier, you have within you seeds of greatness, and the end point of their development is dependent upon the nutrients you take in. These seeds underscore your purpose and as you engage in your purpose your unique ability to share with others will emerge. If we humbly submit to our purpose, I believe we will be better equipped to serve others.

As a metaphor relevant to the above, life is like a musical score that demands to be played; as musicians, we must become completely absorbed so that we may deliver an exceptional performance. As is true of any professional musician, we are required to commit ourselves to the musical score, if it is to be performed as was intended. We are not just to underline the score, but the score must underscore us. Or in other words, our purpose, like the musical score, must be the way we live our lives. It is only by "soaking" ourselves in the true meaning of our purpose that we become intimately familiar with our internal voice and gain a deep, intuitive sense of the many, necessary avenues we must travel. If we follow these paths, we will find ourselves becoming more fruitful as valued members of our communities. This is what "human flourishing" is all about!

Do you doubt that the seeds of greatness within you can lead to the flourishing of yourself and others? If so, please allow me to encourage you with the following interlude. A number of years ago, I read and was deeply impacted by a small book written by Og Mandino titled, *The Greatest Miracle In The World.*[27] I was very inspired by that reading and, while an employee of The Upjohn Company, wrote a brief manuscript titled "A New Day Dawning." The manuscript, which included much of Mandino's writings and one that I could recite from memory, was distributed in booklet form to employees within the company and audiences where I had been invited to speak about a "can do attitude." In that document, I posed the question pertaining to what the future holds for our society. I asked, "What role will you and I play in the shaping of our future?" The following is taken from that booklet:

27. Mandino, Og. *The Greatest Miracle in the World.* reissue ed., Bantam Books, 1988.

As mentioned, we are the last generation of a society that came to an end at the stroke of midnight, thus the first generation of a new society. That which has gone by matters not. Life is what we make it from this moment forward. It is what happens, beginning right now, that is important. There are no more rehearsals. The curtain is going up. The world is watching, waiting to applaud. Life is a Super Bowl—a game to win. Do we have what it takes?

Does the sun rise and fall without our witness? No. We can see—and the hundred million receptors in our eyes enable us to enjoy the magic of a leaf, a child, a rose, a star, a rainbow.

Can a baby cry without our attention? No. We can hear, and the twenty-four thousand fibers built in each ear vibrate to the wind in the trees, the tides on rocks, the majesty of an opera, a robin's plea, children at play.

Do our lips move, yet bring forth no sound? No. We can speak as can no other creature, and our words can calm the angry, uplift the despondent, warm the lonely, praise the worthy, encourage the defeated, teach the ignorant.

Are we paralyzed? No. We can move—run, dance, work—for within us are five hundred muscles, two hundred bones, and seven miles of nerve fiber—all synchronized to do our bidding.

Are we unloved and unloving? Does loneliness engulf us, night and day? No. For we know love's secret that to receive love, it must be given with no thought of its return. Love is a gift. We know that to love unselfishly is its own reward.

Is our heart stricken? Does it leap and strain to maintain life? No. Our heart is strong. Feel its rhythm pulsating, hour after hour, day and night, thirty-six million beats each year, year after year, asleep or awake, pumping our blood through more than sixty thousand miles of veins, arteries, arterioles, and venules—pumping more than six hundred thousand gallons each year. Man has never created such a machine.

Does the breath of life struggle to enter our body? No. Our lungs support us even in the vilest of environments, and they labor always to filter life-giving oxygen through six hundred million pockets of folded flesh while they rid our body of gaseous wastes.

Is our blood poisoned, diluted with water and infection? No. Within our five quarts of blood are twenty-two trillion blood cells and within each cell are millions of molecules and within each molecule is an atom oscillating at more than ten million times each second. Each second, two million of our blood cells die to be replaced by two million more in a resurrection that has continued since birth.

Do people turn in horror when we approach? No. Our skin is clear and a marvel of creation. In time all steels will tarnish and rust, but not our skin. Eventually, the strongest of metals will wear with use, but not that layer constructed around us. Constantly it renews itself, old cells replaced by new. Physically speaking, the entire human body is replaced every eleven months. Think about it.

What about our mind? Can we no longer think for ourselves? No. As already suggested, our brain is the most complex structure in the universe. Within its approximately three pounds are thirteen billion nerve cells, more than three times as many cells as there are people on earth. To help us file every perception, every sound, every taste, every smell, every action we have experienced since the day of our birth, there are implanted, within our cells, more than one thousand billion protein molecules. And, to assist our brain in the control of our body are dispersed, throughout our form, four million pain-sensitive structures, five hundred thousand touch detectors, and more than two hundred thousand temperature detectors. No nation's gold is better protected than we. None of the ancient wonders of the world are greater than we.

Do we have what it takes? You bet. We are The Greatest Miracle in the World.

The earth is ours and the fullness thereof. It's time to set goals worthy of pursuit. It's time to establish the meaning of purpose for our lives, as well as the lives of those around us and the institutions we represent.

Whether you connect with the above notion that we are the greatest miracle in the world or the metaphor of seeds of greatness, the point I am attempting to demonstrate and convince you of is that we have everything within us to become exactly what we are intended to be. Thus, it is of foremost importance that we set our conscious minds upon the task of carefully discerning what our purpose in life shall be, in order to answer "Why am I here?" and then commit to a *humble* attitude that moves us towards that goal.

Baseball's great Tommy Lasorda once said, "There are three kinds of people in this world: people who *make it happen*, people who *watch what happens*, and people who *wonder what happened*."[28] Whether or not an individual accepts it, I believe we are all meant to be the ones who "make it happen." Humble leaders make it happen (with the aid of those who follow) by continuously attempting to answer the question, "Why am I here?" They pay attention to life's happenings and strive to be present each moment. They thoughtfully consider what they observe in the world around them in light of their core values. They actively take part in life when after weighing the merits of this knowledge, they move these principles and life experiences into the heart, where they can be felt and turned into positive words and action. In this way, humble leaders become uniquely equipped to understand and respond to all elements of life, the good and the bad. They recognize that each moment of life presents an opportunity to be inspired, rise to the challenge, and champion others. The weight of this does not overwhelm the humble leader, because they know all they need in

---

28. Lasorda, Tommy. "Tommy Lasorda Quotes." Brainy Quote. https://www.brainyquote.com/quotes/tommy_lasorda_610901.

the darkest part of night is only enough light to make the next step, and if they aim to be just one percent better today than they were yesterday, they will have succeeded. The gift the humble leader enjoys as a result of this is perspective and the untold value of faith. The humble leader is able to truly enjoy all that is positive and uplifting, internalize its influence, and experience lasting personal growth. These positive influences come to dominate the humble leader's perspective and color their vision with a way through a bleak, gray landscape. By choosing to enhance life's flourishing and taking the necessary step of faith, the humble leader transcends labels such as naivete or cynicism as they daily impact the lives around them for the better.

A few years ago, Dave Kerpen, founder and CEO of Likeable Local, published a brief article in *Inc.* titled "The 2 Most Important Days In Your Life." While his comments had to do with leading your company, he included a well-known Mark Twain statement, "The two most important days in your life are the day you were born and the day you find out why."[29] For some of you, Mark Twain's statement may well come across as just another of those canned remarks that we hear over and over again; however, I encourage you to truly ponder the weight of that statement. No doubt, we can accept the importance of our day of birth, but if it is true that life and its essential elements are placed in our care, the importance of "why" becomes exceedingly significant! In her book, *Enduring Edge—Transforming How We Think, Create and Change,* Ms. Amita Shukla writes most winsomely on the sublime importance of seeking and diligently pursuing our individual purpose:

> For most of us, life is truly lived when we travel the raw untrodden paths. In those moments, we discover meaning and feel most alive. Many highways lead to destinations that lose their luster when reached. We travel unaware in a hurry to arrive, only to realize we forget to stop and ask *why* we are on this road to pursue this destination. Fear leads us on some, the ego on others. Yet the secret is to pursue paths with wisdom. We complete many inner journeys

---

29. Kerpen, Dave. "The 2 Most Important Days In Your Life." *Inc.,* July 8, 2013. https://www.inc.com/dave-kerpen/leadership-the-most-important-days-in-your-life.html.

alongside our outer ones, and although the world often doesn't see them, they shape who we become.[30]

With this in mind, learn of your purpose and decide how you will humbly lead yourself and others to flourish in all seasons of life.

The title of this book is *The Miracle of Humble Leadership*. Miracles do occur. Without question, we are The Greatest Miracle in The World. Once we appreciate the value of knowing one's true worth and living an authentic life, it must follow that as we lead ourselves and others, we have every opportunity to be the people who "make it happen"!

Humble leadership is a way of life that is based on one's desire to serve others. It derives from developing inspired, transforming relationships of mutual influence. The relationship pursues shared goals that result in elevating the relationship to higher levels of motivation, morality, and achievement. When included in a larger ethos of mutually benefiting relationships, humble leadership results in a form of cooperation that leads toward increasing levels of excellence, all of which is subordinate to an overarching ethic of general welfare, human flourishing, and moral courage. I have identified that my purpose is to contribute to the flourishing of all in the community in which I exist. To be sure, being an impetus to the flourishing of someone else is a "tall order!" It carries with it the essence of responsibility. Embracing this responsibility is characteristic of the *humble leader* and is an assignment I accept with honor. Join me!

APPLICATION QUESTIONS

- How would you describe the humble leader? Why?

- What are your answers to the following questions regarding the 4 key components of humility?

- Who am I and what value do I place on myself?

---

30. Shukla, Amita. Enduring Edge: Transforming How We Think, Create and Change. Vitamita House, 2014.

- Do I have a positive, productive attitude about forming and maintaining relationships?

- What are my goals when I socialize? Do I find it useful or important to be a member of community and why?

- Can I truly and effectively establish an adaptable and life-giving perspective that reflects the appropriate respect for others?

- Do I describe myself as a humble person, and in what areas do I struggle with being humble (refer to Col. Athens' self assessment)?

- How many close relationships of mutual inspiration can I realistically maintain? Why? How can still I make a useful contribution to other relationships in my community?

- Have you ever witnessed a humble leader making a significant impact on someone else's life? If not, what argument would you present that humble leadership gives rise to miracles?

- Who are you and what is your individual purpose?

CHAPTER 3: Become a Humble Leader:
Take Responsibility for Your Choices

It is imperative for us to accept that every step we take in life is chosen by us, and that we are influenced by our dual nature, good and evil. In chapter one, we unveiled the dark inclination within each of us to make choices that are self-serving and which ultimately destroy flourishing. In chapter two, we discovered that we are also able to choose the humble path that leads to the flourishing of ourselves and others. We must never allow ourselves to forget that both sides of these natures exist, and we therefore must nurture the good within us by surrounding ourselves with positive influences and making choices that faithfully pursue flourishing. We need to recognize that each seemingly insignificant choice has greater impact than we realize, and we must be cognizant of the power we wield, as we are always leading someone, whether formally or completely unbeknownst to us. Thus, we have an incredible responsibility to make sure our choices are in tune with positive action. How frequently do you think about the power you or your words have over someone else? Have you ever made a choice without considering the consequences or its impact?

In the early spring of 2017, I spoke with Vice Admiral Ted Carter, Superintendent of the U. S. Naval Academy, who advised not to make the mistake of thinking leaders and followers are discrete entities:

> As you know, your perspective on leadership gradually becomes clearer and more detailed as you are involved in the effort over many years. If I consider my "leadership" to have begun when I came to the Naval Academy, I have been in this crucible for more

than 40 years. I think my perspective in the early years was pretty simple, that is, you were either a follower or you were a leader. I assumed they were defined as kind of straight lines and thought I would be a follower for most of my time here as a midshipman. What I quickly found out was that there were leaders even in the freshman year. So, my perspective on "leadership" began early on. I aspired to be that leader who reflected the good qualities of the many outstanding role models I observed. As I developed my perspective—and it continues as a work in progress—I have come to know that leadership is all about getting people to do the right thing. While it may not be what's necessarily legally correct, it is about doing the right thing. It is about inspiring the team, giving them trust and confidence, showing them the principles, and then letting them go do it so that they're doing the right thing even when nobody's watching. That defines the high performing team. It's hard to come by—teams that are that good. We were pretty good at that here. Some people say we were good at it, but I know it's a work in progress.

The leadership described here requires one to be aware that someone is always watching and that it is critical to demonstrate principles worthy of emulating. It can be all too easy to assume your behavior and your slip ups don't make an impact because no one will notice.

A pharmaceutical sales representative told me about calling on a physician with the intent of discussing the use of a specific drug to treat diabetes. He was sitting across the desk from the physician, who was holding a *Wall Street Journal* and appeared to have no interest in what was being said. The sales rep, frustrated due to the "lack of attention" he seemed to be getting, closed his comments with, "And this product is a sure cure for cancer." Immediately, the physician dropped the paper, looked the rep directly in his eyes and said, "Don't waste my time, young man! You may think I'm reading this paper but I'm listening to every word you say."

Good decision-making involves knowing and pursuing your purpose despite frustrations. The first mistake the rep made was underestimating the intellectual capabilities of the doctor by believing he was not listening. The second mistake of the careless comment incurred the doctor's wrath, because he disrespected the doctor's time, who doubtless had thirty sick patients waiting to be seen. While the rep's purpose was to promote the use of his product for diabetes, something he knew quite well, he made the wrong assumption based on what he "thought" he knew and let his pride get the better of him.

You are a powerful individual who greatly impacts life's events, so take the time to thoroughly consider the proper choice. If you are committed to becoming someone who facilitates the development and growth of others, your choices are important and demand this thoughtfulness. In Lewis Carroll's *Alice's Adventures in Wonderland*, Alice is faced with this very significance when she comes to a fork in the road:

"Which road do I take?" she asked.
"Where do you want to go?" responded the Cheshire cat.
"I don't know," Alice answered.
"Then," said the cat, "it doesn't matter."[31]

Here Alice learns that her choices only matter if she considers and decides where she wants to go—what her goal or purpose is.

Life is not a parade you watch as it passes by, nor a football game you watch from the bench. You are a key player who must get involved, and establishing your purpose is not easy! When someone of authority comes to you and asks, "Who are you? Why are you here? Where are you going?" What is your answer? If you have accepted the notion that you came into this world as a sovereign individual and are afforded life in a community that respects that sovereignty, what value and responsibility to yourself and others do you assign with that implied freedom? In the end, what will be your legacy?

---

31. Carroll, Lewis. *Alice's Adventures in Wonderland.* Dover Thrift: New York, 1993. The original printing was by the Clarendon Press, Oxford, England in 1865.

When choosing, bravely consider fresh perspectives and, again, make the choice to be thorough and accurate in your assessment of an opportunity and remove "limiting constraints," whether they take the form of custom, habituation, or vices. If you choose to be appropriately informed and step out of these constraints, you will be surprised as to how better equipped you are to pursue the truly meaningful experiences of life. On 4 October 2018, Dr. Jordan Peterson in an interview with Dr. Mehmet Cengiz Oz (Doctor Oz of TV fame) discussed the importance of making the right decisions relative to the true meaning of life. During the interview, he commented on the importance of aiming to have the highest character you can conceptualize, which will give you the moral fortitude to endure during difficult times and to become someone who can be relied upon in a crisis. Therefore, strive to be the secure, inviolable person at a burial ceremony because there are those around you who will not be strong and need someone to turn to, who can share the emotional strength necessary to carry on until the time for grieving has passed.

With the above in mind, you may ask, "How do I become the secure, inviolable person at the burial ceremony, the person to whom others may turn for comfort or consolation? And, the answer is to maintain a constant improvement of your character. Whatever it is today, make it better tomorrow. Listen to your conscience. More than two thousand years ago, Socrates was aware that it is always telling you what you should or shouldn't be doing. And, as history tells us, listening to and following his conscience discriminated him from the middle-of-the-road person.

In light of this extensive interview, one of my takeaways was the implied benefits of removing self-imposed constraints and making the right choice. It is for this reason I want to champion you to take the step to make a few critical decisions—namely, stop doing things that do not serve you well or weaken your potential, and start doing things that will contribute to your flourishing and those whom you lead. I ask you to always tell the truth, which is not as easy as you might think. I ask you to seek to become the individual who lives a rich and fulfilling life. I ask that you treasure the meaningful aspects of life, those of intrinsic value that are inherently moral and have a purpose. I ask that you accept the responsibility that you are a leader and are fully aware of all that leadership entails.

From my early twenties and for more than six years, I was a very heavy smoker before finally giving up the habit. I consumed sixty to eighty cigarettes per day (I smoked all day and half the night). I also smoked an occasional cigar and, from time to time, a pipe (primarily for show). I thoroughly enjoyed the habit—no yellow fingers, no coughing—just the pleasure of a little immediate stimulation followed by short-lived relaxation.

In 1962, I had decided to leave the practice of pharmacy to take a sales position with The Upjohn Company. In my third year with the company and second sales assignment, I found myself in a professional clinic located in Winter Park, Florida. The clinic housed nine physicians and support staff. Most of the physicians and staff adhered to beliefs of the Seventh Day Adventist Church and one of the Church's beliefs prohibited smoking tobacco. Therefore, smoking was not permitted in the clinic, and that was a significant problem for anyone with a serious habit.

This was an important clinic for me. All the physicians specialized in Internal Medicine, were potential users of a number of my company's drugs, saw many patients every day, and the majority of patients would need at least one prescription. It was also important because it was an efficient use of my time. While it was not unusual to wait an hour or more to call on one physician and then take additional time to drive to the next office, I could arrive at this clinic at eight o'clock in the morning and have made nine individual, high-value calls by noon. There was only one problem—no smoking from eight o'clock until noon!

Two weeks before this particular Monday, I, who considered myself a "clotheshorse in development," had purchased a new, Hart Schaffner Marx suit made of wool and mohair, a suit I couldn't afford at the time. I was showing off this suit when I called on physicians and other personnel in the clinic. As usual, I arrived early, endured the "no smoking" requirement, and returned to the car shortly after noon. At last, I could have a smoke!

Just as I lit the cigarette, a spark from the match fell to the left leg of my slacks and burned a small hole, just above the knee and at the crease. Since the burn was on the crease, I was told that reweaving was not an option and there was no chance of disguising the damage. I, the to-be "clotheshorse," was devastated.

Now, you may question why I had such a strong reaction to this "accident," so here it is. I was young and inexperienced, and all of my clients were older with significant experience. While I held a degree in pharmacy, many years of experience as a pharmacist, and felt appropriately trained to discuss methods of treating certain illnesses with pharmaceuticals, the majority of my clients (pharmacists, physicians, nurses) were equally educated, and many had advanced academic degrees. Since my job, in most cases, was to "stop" these professionals from doing what they were doing to care for their patients and "start" doing what I had decided was better, I felt I needed every advantage I could come up with to gain an audience so that I could tell my story—image was one such advantage.

To be sure, looking back on that experience, I was probably close to being obsessed with the "need" to make a good impression, and the value I placed on "perfection" was unrealistic. However, I held the notion at that time, and continue to this day, that what people see initially, before we speak the first word, is important when attempting to establish a relationship.

The above experience marked the beginning of the end of a well-developed smoking habit for me. For the reader who has broken the habit or is close to someone else who has, you are well aware of the difficulty! While I will not describe the extensive process through which I went to give it up, know that that was the end—no smoking at all from then until this day!

Suffice it to say, if it is important enough, and you will know, make the right decision and do it now!

I was thirty years of age when I had my first real taste of alcohol. The drink was "rum and coke" because someone had told me that it was a good drink for beginners. As I recall, it went down fairly well, and after a few passing moments and a little small talk with friends, the second went down even better. That was the beginning of many years of drinking. Social drinking and the daily "five o'clock happy hour" became common to my way of life. There was a time when I thought I could drink all the alcohol produced, but I eventually learned the fallacy of alcohol-induced courage.

Years later, on a Sunday morning in the early 2000s, a member of the Protestant Choir and participant in the Holy Communion Service at the United States Naval Academy Chapel asked me if I would help with the Holy Communion Service. I, who rarely say no when asked to serve, said, "Yes… I will do whatever you ask if it will serve the chapel staff and members of the congregation." It was an honor to be asked. And, frankly, I was a bit "puffed up." For a brief moment I thought that living the "ideal church-goers" life—dressing the part, being a regular attendee of the Sunday-morning services, being on time, saying the right thing at the right time, along with many other "rights"—had paid off again! It wasn't until I had given honest thought to what had been asked of me and why I had agreed to do it that I came to this conclusion that rather than aiming to serve others, I was after my own glorification.

Of even greater importance, I also came to the conclusion that the life I was living did not reflect the true meaning of that which Holy Communion represents—the Life, Death, and Resurrection of Jesus Christ. That is to say, I could not stand before a fellow member of the church body and proclaim that the elements—the bread and wine—I was handing them represented the body of my Savior broken for us and the blood of my Savior poured out for us, while trying to overcome a headache due to my choices the night before.

After this personal assessment and reflection on my commitment to the flourishing of others, the decision to participate in Holy Communion Services marked the beginning of the end of my "It's five o'clock somewhere" lifestyle. Once I came to grips with the notion that my "five o'clock ritual" created a physical weakness and emotional dependence that did not, nor would ever serve me well, it became abundantly clear that it was time to stop. It was time to make a choice, it was time to make a decision: Stop! Choose a new direction.

What is the message? If it is important enough, and you will know, make the decision and do it now!

As stated at the beginning of this message, I will ask you to make a few decisions, directly and by implication—*stop doing things that don't serve you well—they make you weak—and start doing things that will serve you and others well.* In Shakespeare's *Macbeth*, we read:

> Life's but a walking shadow, a poor player
> That struts and frets his hour upon the stage
> And then is heard no more. It is a tale
> Told by an idiot, full of sound and fury,
> Signifying nothing.[32]

Thus, I pose the questions: Are we manipulative, mildly narcissistic beings who exist only to serve our own needs? Are we our name, our accomplishments, our worldly possessions, our titles, trophies, triumphs, or our tragedies? These treasures we seek and attempt to cling to are temporary and transient. They may have at one point promised value and permanence, but time and time again these lesser goods have been sources of immense personal and communal suffering. In the end, if we allow lesser vain desires to rule us then we will agree with Macbeth—life is a shadow. We will wholeheartedly believe that there is nothing original in our life and we have nothing to offer.

I hope this will not be just another book you read. I hope you take all that is presented and transfer it from an intellectual understanding to a heart-directed way of life that engenders a joyously-inspired personal life for you, the reader, and all whom you encounter now and forever!

---

32. Shakespeare, William. *Macbeth*. Folger Shakespeare Library. Act 5, Scene 5, lines 24-28.

Humble leadership is exceedingly important. Stop doing what doesn't serve you well, and make the transformation necessary to become a Humble Leader.

As we go further, you will find that "the miracle of humble leadership" does not come without a price! To be sure, there will be times of felt darkness, where life's journey is difficult and fraught with fatigue and hardship with the ever-present challenge to quit. In this world you, the humble leader, will experience trouble and suffering. Even though these are not exactly the cheery words you want to hear, and while at times they deliver what will be the absolute truth, be of good courage, they are not the words that reflect the endpoint! Keep in mind that you have no idea of the strength of your capabilities and the following stories are a couple of examples that represent that very fact.

For more than five decades, many of our young people have *chosen* to serve in our Country's Peace Corps. As volunteers in 141 countries, they have demonstrated ingenuity, creativity, and grit to solve critical challenges alongside community leaders. Do you know anyone who is currently serving or has served in the Peace Corps? I do and can assure you, it is no "casual walk in the park!" The young people who have made this choice often represent the humble leadership I hope to establish through writing this book. I have included an abbreviated list of requirements of each Peace Corps Volunteer to impress upon you the level of humility and sacrifice of these men and women:

1. Prepare your personal and professional life to make a commitment to serve abroad for a full term of 27 months.

2. Commit to improving the quality of life of the people with whom you live and work; and, in doing so, share your skills, adapt them, and learn new skills as needed.

3. Serve where the Peace Corps asks you to go, under conditions of hardship, if necessary, and with the flexibility needed for effective service.

4. Recognize that your successful and sustainable development work is based on the local trust and confidence you build by living in, and respectfully integrating yourself into, your host community and culture.

5. Recognize that you are responsible 24 hours a day, 7 days a week for your personal conduct and professional performance.

6. Engage with host country partners in a spirit of cooperation, mutual learning, and respect.

7. Work within the rules and regulations of the Peace Corps and the local and national laws of the country where you serve.

8. Exercise judgment and personal responsibility to protect your health, safety, and well-being and that of others.

9. Recognize that you will be perceived, in your host country and community, as a representative of the people, cultures, values, and traditions of the United States of America.

10. Represent responsibly the people, cultures, values, and traditions of your host country and community to people in the United States both during and following your service.[33]

Anyone who meets the above qualifications is a likely candidate for almost any "cushy" job our country has to offer. They could easily earn an income to provide comfortable housing, pretty clothes, good food—all that we refer to as the "good life." Knowing this, why do they choose the difficulties and hardships inherent in countries rampant with corruption, widespread poverty and a life expectancy known to be less than that of our own homeland? Could it be a sincere, humble focus on others and their needs?

Another such example of a seemingly undesirable but worthy choice will be familiar to those who have ever walked the Campus of Washington University in Seattle or read the great book *Boys in the Boat* by Daniel

---

33. "Core Expectations for Peace Corps Volunteers," Peace Corps. https://www.peacecorps.gov/volunteer/is-peace-corps-right-for-me/peace-corps-volunteer/core-expectations-peace-corps-volunteers/.

James Brown. On this campus you will find an advertisement intended to recruit boys for the rowing team. Unlike what one would expect for a recruiting ad, an ad that highlighted the thrill of recognition and honor that comes with success, it seemed to use words that emphasized just the opposite—cold, darkness, fatigue, hardship—words that did not emphasize the "bright" side and inspire one to join the team.

For those of you who read the book or know a little about this team, you will recall their experience was often marked with drama and moments of agony but also with those of absolute exhilaration of achievement. Perhaps most notable is the story of their quest for gold at the 1936 Berlin Olympics: an eight-oar crew who was not expected to compete successfully against even the East Coast American teams at the time showed astonishing strength, providing a winning story that would not be forgotten.

Based on the words in the advertisement, it is unlikely that the U of W's freshmen chose to be on the school's rowing team because it was all that rewarding. Even though there existed the possibility of glory in triumph, that was not the compelling point. There had to be something else because, among other things, there was an obvious cost! What was promised was pain and sacrifice, and we may ask, why was this the crew's appeal? Could it be that deep inside these students was a level of courage and commitment that said: "We will endure the pain to achieve something that has never been achieved before"? But let's be honest; some of us would've done this just to brag to our girlfriends. You decide!

The type of young people who made these choices—choices that demonstrate highly valued qualities such as courage, commitment, dedication, and the like—often represent the humble leadership I hope to establish through writing this book.

A few years ago, I had the privilege of meeting Ms. Shukla; listening to her lecture, I was captivated by her description of a life, which expands our thought process. As I listened, I was wondering if one pays that much attention to life as it is lived, if he or she thinks about it influencing their thoughts, or if so, does it make any difference? Although it was unknown to them at the time, the UW boys who chose to be members of the rowing team chose a life that would influence their thinking for the remainder of their lives. The question is, did they give enough attention to their lives as they were being lived and the influence these lives had on their thinking? Life often passes by without much attention and thinking, and many often experience the same fate.

From time to time I hear someone say, "I don't know what I think until I hear myself say it." Likewise, I have an acquaintance who does a great deal of public speaking. He often says he sits in the room backstage, thinks about what he wants to say, something he thinks will be useful to the audience, and eventually comes up with a topic. His thinking is based on the life he has lived, which includes the work he has done—readings, discussions, research—and the thoughts he has developed. After reaching the stage and beginning his presentation, he carefully watches the audience for an early response, which gives some evidence that he is or is not on the right track or is beginning with something that has gotten the audience's attention. By sharing his thoughts with a "critical audience," he is able to assess their validity, which is important to confirming his continuation of his personal and professional life as is or should there be a change. As an aside, there have been times when I have approached the stage the same way. Even though I knew in advance the message I wanted to deliver, the approach was never the same two times in a row, and it reminds me a little of life in that we may know, in general, what the day is to bring, but as we give it a little thought, it may be approached quite differently.

The point of the foregoing is that much of life is a "trial and error" experience, and if one pays careful attention, it can forge new paths of living. Therefore, pay careful attention to results, so that you can determine whether an "on the fly" approach will be useful. In some sense, life comes and goes like a public speech! One has some idea as to how it should turn out but doesn't actually know until its path has been followed.

I have said before that one's purpose is not easily discovered, and even less easily pursued. Life has a tendency to throw up countless obstacles in the way of powerful movements and epic journeys. This being the case we should prepare for the difficulties that will come our way and live each day as Shukla advises, not in perpetual draft mode, but rather put forth our very best, as if it will be recorded as part of our own legends. Exercise the wisdom you have sought, put it into action, and let the world adjust to you.

"Humble leadership" is a way of life, a life of courage, character, and truth! As is suggested by *Alice in Wonderland*, it is characterized by knowing which "fork in the road" to take. It derives from inspiring, transforming relationships of mutual influence where the leader and led reach higher levels of morality, motivation, and achievement. It assures all of us that hope, honor, and recognition come with this success. Herein is the glory of triumph—everyone wins!

The first step in leading is to recognize that we lead ourselves first. We must have a clearly established purpose for our lives and make every effort to achieve that purpose every day. Second, we must remain committed to the bigger picture and remove our limiting constraints, whether that be close-minded thinking or habits that hobble us in pursuit of our purpose. And finally, recognize that our every act, spoken and written word leads someone. Someone is watching and listening and will be led in one direction or another. Make sure it is right! As we move to the next chapter, we will analyze character studies of humble leaders who have walked the road before. By studying the morals and virtues that fuel their ability to serve humbly, we will know what changes we need to make to our own character to best prepare us for such a life.

APPLICATION QUESTIONS

- How does our dual nature influence our decision-making and how we determine what habits will serve us well?

- How do we make sure our choices communicate respect for others?

- Which of your own habits are at best unproductive or at worst antagonistic to your flourishing and that of those around you? Do you remember when this habit initially began, and has your assessment of this choice changed? What positive habit could replace this lesser one?

• What is your conception of a worthy challenge? Does your sense of personal purpose prepare you to encounter and overcome difficulties? Do you think challenges make you a more humble leader, and, if so, why?

PART II
Core Virtues of the Humble Leader

CHAPTER 4: Grounds for Enduring Greatness: *Faith, Hope, Love, Humility, and Compassion*

The next several chapters we will discuss the virtues and skills of leaders who are worthy of our emulation. I have worked with numerous professionals over the years who occupied key positions of leadership in a variety of institutions. Titles for these positions were varied and included group directors, group managers, and division managers. During interviews with these individuals, their levels of success seemed to have less to do with meeting job requirements and more to do with the virtues that were distinguishing characteristics of the individual. They sought out places of employment and communities that were pursuing worthwhile goals, and they became what their institutions needed in order to be the best. In this chapter, we will tackle the essential traits I believe to be core to humble leadership in any arena. Or in other words, if you begin to treasure these principles and exhibit them in your everyday lives, many other positive traits will follow naturally. I selected these traits because they are the ones re-emphasized again and again by those successful leaders who best exemplify this book's definition of humble leadership. Therefore, it appears to me that the clearest path to becoming such a leader is to seek to understand these traits with the purpose of making them a way of life so that we will put them into practice in our every word and action. As you read through these virtues, consider people in your life who have succeeded or failed to exhibit that virtue, assess its value both in terms of short and long term impact, and how it affects one's sphere of influence. Is this virtue worth the choice to live it out each day?

In this chapter, we will analyze five virtues: faith, hope, love, humility, and compassion, as I believe they are best comprehended in relation to each other and mastering these essential five is necessary to the development of the subsequent virtues.

Faith

As we begin our discussion of this important trait, I ask that you make every effort to accept the objective truth that our brain is the most powerful computer known and the most complex system ever studied. The consciousness (that stage when we are attentive, perceptive and aware of our feelings and surroundings) and the intelligence of our minds has the power to permeate and affect every cell of our body, thus every bodily system. Our mind and its unlimited power are nature's most astonishing creation. Without a doubt, the importance of one's thoughts must not be underestimated since they have a far-reaching impact on the entirety of one's life.

With the foregoing in mind, we embrace the idea that *faith is a thought or collection of thoughts*, whatever the source, that we will weigh in comparison with our other thoughts and will have the ability to affect our activities. Faith, thoughts in which we believe, is the impetus, power, or energy that ignites one's spirit. This spirit paves the way to the development of attitudes that execute plans of action and affect the way we react to situations. Said another way, faith can be the driving force behind all that is good for one's life, but it depends upon what one places their faith in—is it the true, the good, and the beautiful? As we continue our discussion of faith, let's remember the words of Napoleon Hill, "Whatever the mind can conceive and believe, the mind can achieve."[34]

Development of faith is a lifetime process. As a child, I remember Mom saying, "Have faith; everything will work out," but for me, one who was expecting instant gratification, that statement was meaningless. To my young mind, faith was an *intangible*, something I couldn't see or touch. It was

34. "Napoleon Hill Quotes." BrainyQuote.com. BrainyMedia Inc, 2020. 7 April 2020. https://www.brainyquote.com/quotes/napoleon_hill_392258.

immersed in mystery, too much for me to comprehend, and it wasn't until I became older and saw a few results of faith that I could give it any level of appreciation.

You may relate to my younger self and have difficulty understanding and seeing the value in faith. This faith came about through years of often unintentional training. The infant who could have faith that his mother will feed him, rather experiences more immediate satisfaction when faith is supplanted by crying. From this very early stage, our brain is undergoing a period of rapid change and is developing more than at any other time in life. To be sure, it makes an excess of a million neural connections each second in response to influences from many factors including relationships, experiences and environment. Furthermore, these factors that influence us, whether they are positive or negative, have a lasting impact on a child's life and choices. Depending on these factors, continued development of faith or the lack thereof will determine the likelihood of one being able to effectively work with the unknown and establish a behavioral pattern that yields success and reward.

One of the challenges we face relates to the likelihood of our accepting mental transformation, that is, the extent to which we are willing to renew our way of thinking about faith. To be sure, faith has the ability to sustain an alert, abiding awareness of life as it passes by and a determination to live it as an active participant. We must accept the notion that our life moves toward our dominant thoughts. Even though we cannot eliminate mentally recorded events of the past and their impact on us, we can override them with our thoughts for the future, and thus impact our lives going forward. We know that life is difficult and will challenge us with many intellectual and emotional disappointments. It is when these disappointments come our way that we, as humble leaders, must remember that a strong and courageous faith is the order of the day, and a mature attitude that embodies the truth that all things, good or bad, work together for a better tomorrow. While I had reason to be skeptical of faith as an uninformed, impetuous child, I am no longer a child and those who follow me have every reason to expect nothing less than my best!

As an aside, for those of you who have a little difficulty accepting this line of thinking, keep reading. In the following section on hope, I provide good evidence that faith has a tangible existence with supporting scientific evidence developed in the biological laboratory.

The King James translation of Hebrews states, "Now faith is the substance of things hoped for, the evidence of things not seen."[35] As the substance of things hoped for, faith is given tangible existence here in this verse, and furthermore, it is given the privilege of place as an anchor for our hopes. Gallup's findings reinforce this notion—they found that hope is one of the four reasons that people will follow you.[36] Hope is powerful and not to be underestimated. Next we see that faith is given intellectual concreteness and value as being compared to evidence of those things that are unseen. Hebrews will not allow us to relegate faith to the realm of the wishy washy dreams of little girls. James W. Fowler, once a Professor of Theology and Human Development at Emory University, stated, "Faith is an orientation of the total person, giving purpose and goal to one's hopes and strivings, thoughts and actions."[37] A sense of purpose and a goal that is clearly defined and boldly pursued by an individual makes things happen. Be respectful of others' strivings! In Fowler's book, *Stages of Faith*, he presents his idea of a development process in "human faith" and this process is similar to Jean Piaget's theory of cognitive development.[38] While this literature is not necessarily germane to our brief focus on faith, his four states of learning will be discussed briefly a little later on and a few words concerning Piaget's theory may be useful.

Piaget worked with infants, children, and adolescents and identified four stages in cognitive development: the *sensorimotor stage*, which includes the years birth to age two and is the period during which the infant demon-

---

35. Hebrews 11:1. KJV.

36. Rath, Tom, and Barry Conchie. *Strengths Based Leadership: Great Leaders, Teams, and Why People Follow*. Gallup Press, 2009.

37. Fowler, James W. *Stages of Faith: The Psychology of Human Development and the Quest for Meaning*. San Francisco: Harper & Row, 1981.

38. Huitt, W., & Hummel, J. (2003). "Piaget's Theory of Cognitive Development." Valdosta, GA: Valdosta State University. *Edpsycinteractive.com, 10 April 2020*, http://www.edpsycinteractive.org/topics/cognition/piaget.html.

strates intelligence through basic reflexes, senses, and motor responses; the *preoperational stage*, which includes the years two through seven, is when intelligence is demonstrated through the child's ability to think about things symbolically—pretend play, drawing, writing, and speaking; the *concrete operational stage*, which includes years seven to eleven, is that period during which the child begins to think more logically and understand that their thoughts are unique to them and that not everyone else necessarily shares their thoughts, feelings, and opinions; and lastly, the *formal operational stage*, which begins at age twelve and continues throughout adulthood, is the period when the individual begins to think in an abstract form and applies reasoning to general to specific information.

As you think about faith as the substance of things hoped for, the evidence of things not seen, you can understand why Fowler stated the development process of "human faith" will naturally follow the stages of Piaget's theory of cognitive development. Since faith is composed of intentional thoughts, the process of developing faith must begin as any other thought; we may not see the results of our efforts in the early phases but as time passes and we mature, experience is gained, richness of our faculties is deepened, and the results become more evident. As said earlier, the remarkable power of the mind is always such that it moves life toward our dominant thoughts. Once the seed of faith is planted and nutrition in the form of affirmation is provided, positive results accumulate.

Our late President Ronald Reagan made famous the statement, "Trust, but verify." This caveated trust is not exemplifying true faith, and while humble leaders should strive to put their faith in the true, good, and beautiful things without constant need for verification themselves, they must recognize that their followers may not accept their decision or assessment without verification and give room for this.

Faith is indeed a catalyst for emergence of biological factors that can be measured in the laboratory or seen under a microscope; these factors prepare and attune us to accomplish the feat. Beyond the laboratory, we see evidence of the power of faith in the world at large in the achievements of mankind. The humble leader accepts this truth and will fight to sustain their own faith and the faith of those around them, and I have no doubt that they will experience a result worthy of that faith. In the end, how much one desires to have faith will determine the extent to which it will come their way. Do you really want to have faith? Dismiss your prejudices, whatever they are, and reach out. It is there for the taking!

Hope

Hope is one of our many emotions, and as said previously, Rath's and Conchie's study, *Strengths-Based Leadership: Great Leaders, Teams, and Why People Follow*, identifies hope as one of the four primary motivators for others to follow us. It is an optimistic state of mind, founded on experiences that resulted in positive outcomes in the past and thereby encourages us to expect, with some degree of confidence, similar results in the future. Amruta Khanvilkar (Malhotra) a young, Indian actress, once wrote, "I am closest to my mother, as she is my rock, my pillar of strength, and my world. Not only has she stood by me through all times—happy, sad, and otherwise—but there have even been moments when I had completely lost hope, and her immense belief in me had lifted me up."[39] I know of few leaders who can compete with mothers on the trait, hope. As we reflect on the immense influence a mother's hope has on a child, we will recognize it is an asset worth pursuing.

Dr. Timothy Keller delivered a speech to students at the University of Hong Kong (HKU) titled, "Hope Beyond the Walls of the World."[40] Early in this speech, he referred to a small book written by Andrew Delbanco and stated: "The heart of any culture is hope. Hope is the way we overcome the lurking suspicion that all our getting and spending amounts to fidgeting while we wait for death. We must imagine some end of life that transcends our own tiny allotment of days and hours if we are to keep at bay the dim back-of-the-mind suspicion that one may be adrift in an absurd

---

39. "Amruta Khanvilkar Quotes." BrainyQuote.com, 5 December 2019. https://www.brainyquote.com/quotes/amruta_khanvilkar_868706.

40. Keller, Timothy. "Hope Beyond the Walls of the World." Youtube, 5 April 2014. https://www.youtube.com/watch?v=SD5LYJ3us0U.

world."[41] In other words, we must overcome the nagging suspicion that life is pointless, that nothing we do matters, that nothing we do has any kind of meaning. Life is not pointless, and we must overcome this suspicion, live life, and do so abundantly—hope makes life meaningful.

The hopeful humble leader is optimistic and provides hope for the future and the expectation of its fulfillment. This leader makes a person enthusiastic, yet realistic about tomorrow and the good things to come. An example of this is the impact Viktor Frankl had on his fellow Holocaust prisoners, as he described in his landmark book, *Man's Search for Meaning*.[42] Frankl, an Austrian neurologist and psychiatrist, promoted the idea that people are goal-oriented and must find meaning in life regardless of circumstances. In the prison camps, Frankl noticed that hope was a distinctive feature between those that were able to survive and those who were not, and thus, sought to inspire hope in his fellow prisoners. In his book, he encouraged a focus on love, responsibility, inner freedom, and the beauty to be found in both nature and art as a means to help one endure and overcome harrowing experiences. To be sure, these are choices one makes to have hope and, as an unknown author once wrote, "Between stimulus and response there is a space. In that space is our power to choose our response. In our response lies our growth and our freedom."

The work of Dr. Bruce H. Lipton,[43] a highly acclaimed cell biologist; Dr. Robert Schneider, a physician focused on internal medicine; and the late Dr. Candice B. Pert,[44] a neuroscientist and pharmacologist who discovered the opiate receptor, which is the cellular binding site for endorphins in the brain; suggests that one's thoughts, as well as other factors, cause the release of a ligand(s), which is a substance in the human's body that forms a complex with another substance that gives rise to a special biological response.

41. Delbanco, Andrew. *The Real American Dream: a Meditation on Hope.* Cambridge, Harvard University Press, 2000.

42. Frankl, Viktor E. *Man's Search for Meaning: An Introduction to Logotherapy.* New York. Simon & Schuster, 1984.

43. Lipton, Bruce. *The Biology of Belief: Unleashing the Power of Consciousness, Matter and Miracles.* Carlsbad, Hay House, 2005.

44. Pert, Candace B. Ph. D. *Molecules of Emotion.* New York, Scribner, 1997.

What I am trying to say is that our thoughts cause certain factors, only some of which have been identified, to be produced and released in the body as a response. A simple example of this is the "fight-flight reaction" we learned about in high school. That is, when faced with the possibility of a gunshot injury, the biological substances released stimulate all systems that are necessary to perform the appropriate reaction. Another example is the "runner's high" normally associated with long-distance runners. This phenomenon, often associated with pain and referred to as an emotion, results from the brain's recognition of the painful condition that influences the release of endorphins, the naturally occurring morphines. All of this is to say that when one's hope is for a better future, biological mechanisms are set into motion that move one in the direction of his or her dominant thoughts. The humble leader provides the physical and social setting in which realistic, justifiable hope may be planted and its continued growth assured.

I recommend you read the works of Drs. Lipton, Pert, Schneider, and others if you are interested in a greater understanding of the many advances that have taken place in the laboratory and help us understand the extreme value of "mind over matter, the mind-body relationships." Hope allows us to approach problems and reach suitable resolutions, and to develop a mindset that permits successful attainment of important goals. So, it is important to know that hope is not simply something that comes to mind from time to time, but something that influences bodily functions. Once we understand our very biology can be influenced by our thoughts, then we can appreciate the value of a humble leader who encourages hope in others.

I mentioned above that the humble leader who is intentionally hopeful is optimistic and encourages others to set hopeful and realistic expectations about the future. For example, if you check into a hotel and the hotel's agent, who is escorting you to your room, describes it as one of great beauty and exceptional amenities, your hope is elevated and justified once he opens the door and his description is realized. You expected something terrific and that is what you got! On the other hand, if, after the same description, you walk into a room that is quite small with a view of a brick wall outside one window and parking lot outside the other, your hope crumbles and you are sorely disappointed. What you expected, based on the description, is not realized. This latter case is a good example of "false hope" that was set by an unrealistic expectation.

Remember, merely expecting something to happen will not make it happen. Children who often base their expectations on subjective assessments of the world around them frequently experience disappointment because their expectations are unrealistic. As the child gets older and their observations are more objective, their expectations become more realistic, and outcomes are closer to what was expected. As stated above, hope must be realistic and when it is, it will be proven justified, but unfortunately, some of us do not fully develop an objective view of the world. The *Law of Attraction* argues that our thoughts invite certain events into our lives, regardless of objectivity, and many of us place significant credence in that *Law*. Another issue is the often-misunderstood relationship between happiness and joy. Happiness is closely related to external factors that are not necessarily under one's control, and joy is related to internal factors within the human body where one has essentially complete control. Those of us who pin our hopes on happiness often risk disappointment, because of the variability of the external factors.

To be sure, expectations are critical to building hope for the future and all expectations must be based on good reasons for that expectation. The leader, who attempts to provide appropriate direction, guidance, and makes a major effort to encourage faith, will infuse his or her followers with tangible confidence that they really know they have what it takes to make the next step. When a leader infuses hopes in others that are based on anticipation of realistic outcomes (i.e. they can see a solution that directly resolves the issue at hand), the leader will have successfully created genuine enthusiasm in his followers about the future.

How does the humble leader develop hope in themselves and thereby others? The following daily practices can be utilized to become more hopeful today than one was yesterday.

1. Acknowledge your strengths.

2. Cultivate supportive relationships.

3. Engage in pleasurable activities.

4. Get involved with a cause.

5. Put yourself in more diverse situations.

6. Keep track of your thoughts and feelings in a journal.

7. Take care of yourself.

Compassion

Compassion, according to the results of Rath's and Conchie's study, *Strengths-Based Leadership: Great Leaders, Teams, and Why People Follow*[45], is one of the four primary reasons why a given individual or group will follow others. It is that quality that motivates people to go "above and beyond the call of duty" to help the physical, mental, or emotional pains of others. The person with this quality is sensitive to the challenges of their fellow men and is caring, understanding, and desirous of lending aid. He or she holds mature, intellectual and emotional regard for all pain and suffering, and operates from a foundation based on cerebral-learned notions such as fairness, justice, understanding, sound judgement and interdependence. Sincere compassion is foundational to deep relationships and as such, it eats up time in our days, as we seek to truly understand and feel another's pain as our own. Without such commitment and sacrifice, compassion becomes weak "niceness"; it cares from a distance and has little to no appreciation of the pain another is suffering and therefore is often entirely incapable of meeting the physical, let alone emotional, needs of the other. To understand compassion, one must understand the difference between empathy, sympathy, and pity.

---

45. Rath, Tom, and Barry Conchie. *Strengths-Based Leadership: Great Leaders, Teams, and Why People Follow*. Gallup Press, 2009.

Empathy may come easily when two individuals share a very similar pain or hardship. More commonly, it is an emotional feeling someone shares with someone else, a feeling that comes to surface when one has walked a mile in another's shoes. It is that feeling which emerges when one moves from the propositional to an experiential, personal, relational knowledge of another person and his or her situation. Empathy can be a very positive, special gift shared between two individuals, but it is birthed from shared circumstance. Nevertheless, this requires significant time and interest in the other person.

Sympathy is a desire to come alongside and attempt to feel another's pain even without personal experience with the same pain. I knew a young man whose office mate was battling cancer and undergoing chemotherapy. In the course of her treatments, she lost her hair and as one might imagine was greatly grieved by this. Her officemate, the young man, although he could not empathize with battling cancer directly, he compassionately desired to sympathize with her; this choice motivated him to shave his head, so he could experience her grief in this way. Sympathy is the choice to strive to feel and understand another's pain. Empathize where you can, but always seek to sympathize!

Be careful that well-intentioned sympathy does not dissolve into fruitless pity. Pity is an attitude of mercy that we bestow on those whom we feel to be less advantaged than ourselves. While pity may show some resemblance to compassion, the fact that pity stems from mercy automatically implies that we believe the suffering individual is in some way responsible for their pitiable state; lurking behind these feelings of benevolence are prideful thoughts like "They could've worked harder like me" or "I would never have done that." Sympathy descends into pity through a lack of imagination and humility. An example of pity is found in the Bible's story of Job and is clearly exemplified by his friends who come to visit him in his wretched state. They are impaired in their ability to comfort Job or truly come alongside him, because they believed he had somehow earned his turn of fortunes. Not only does pity rarely connect us with the suffering individual in any meaningful way, it rarely motivates us to encourage them and attempt to lift them out of their condition; it remains stagnant.

You may have also observed that some people desire to be pitied. Your attempts to connect and encourage them are often rejected; they have found an identity as a victim. It is important for the humble leader to be conscious of these desires and choose the more difficult road of compassion by continuing to encourage them to move beyond victimhood and help them create a better life. Showing pity can be dangerous because it can sometimes worsen an individual's feelings of sorrow and draw him towards feelings of depression and self-pity. I've already proved that "You move toward your dominant thoughts," and you may have heard it stated, "You are what you think." Thoughts create beliefs and are the strongest and most useful powers one may possess. Thus, some individuals, steeped in negative thoughts and experiences, may feel victimized wherever they go, even in the face of contrary evidence. The humble leader will recognize this condition and will patiently and gracefully attempt to convince such an individual that they need not be afraid, that they are safe, respected, etc. It may take years for them to come to see the world around them without the haze of victimhood, but do not give up faith that you can make a difference in their worldview. You may be tempted to follow the easy road and simply agree with their pessimistic thoughts and unrealistic perception, winsomely persuade them of a fuller, more flourishing view of their life. Avoid the easy way out! Seek ways to help others emerge from these conditions or moments of distress, rather than prolonging them by exhibiting pity.

The compassionate, humble leader is invested in the deeper interests and well-being of colleagues, considers the needs, feelings, and concerns of others, and importantly, makes an effort to know others at all levels: superiors, "equals," and subordinates.

As I describe the essence of compassion, my friend, Tom Nees, comes to mind. He is one of the most compassionate people I know. He is a graduate of Northwest Nazarene University, Nazarene Theological Seminary, and Wesley Theological Seminary, where he earned his Doctor of Ministry degree. He is a blogger, writer, and speaker on trends, books, and current events addressing leadership, justice, and compassion. During one of our many conversations, I asked him to relate his experience as a pastor that gave rise to his spending so much time in DC. The Washington, DC riots of 1968 were four days of absolute turmoil that followed the assassination of civil rights activist Dr. Martin Luther King Jr. on April 4, 1968. Approximately three years after these riots, in 1971, Tom became pastor of the First Church of the Nazarene, Washington, DC. During his time as pastor of the "First Church," he became affiliated with Jubilee Housing. Founded in 1973 by the Church of the Savior, Jubilee Housing is a non-profit organization that addresses critical, low-income housing issues in the Columbia Heights neighborhood on Columbia Road NW, Washington, DC. Its mission is to build diverse, compassionate communities that create opportunities for everyone to thrive. In 1973, under Tom's direction, Jubilee Housing acquired a fully occupied, deteriorating 48-unit building at 1430 Belmont Street NW. The residents eventually took ownership of the building as the first low-income coop with assistance for renovation and building management from Jubilee Housing, Inc. As a part of this affiliation, he became involved with the Potter House and the Potter House's mission group, which included Church of the Savior founder, Pastor Gordon Crosby. The Potter House is a rustic, church-run coffee house that is now a vibrant center for activism, the arts, and community development. In 1973, Tom and a few others took responsibility for one of the riot-damaged buildings in the DC area (1430 Belmont St. NW) and began what we know today as the Community of Hope, Inc., a faith-based neighborhood development agency with programs addressing a wide range of needs in the inner city, including homelessness, healthcare, after-school education, job training, legal aid and cultural awareness. In 1975, the Community of Hope took possession of a vacated 24-unit building at 1417 Belmont St. It became the site for transitional housing for homeless families and other neighborhood programs including health services, job training, legal aid and after-school educational assistance. While the Potter House was the venue for services until 1977, this building became the worship site for the Community of Hope Church of the Nazarene.

At the end of one of our discussions, I asked Tom the question: "How did you and your colleagues become a 'welcomed part' of the neighborhood?" His answer: "As a predominately white group engaged in ministry in the African American inner-city neighborhood we had a lot to learn. What we found early on was that the neighborhood was very welcoming when they realized that we were trustworthy and were there to partner with them rather than take over the neighborhood for development." How did Tom prove his trustworthiness? For the first year or two, every day he sat on his front steps outside of the building of which he had taken responsibility. What is the glorious compassion in this act? He was deeply concerned with getting to know the community he wished to serve, and he made himself accessible. He did not come in on a white horse, lecturing on what needed to be changed, throwing money at projects he deemed worthy, or knocking down what was there to make way for his own vision. He humbly observed the community and encouraged them to tell him who they were and what in him could be of use. Tom Nees recognized that he would be viewed as foreign to this community, and thus, prioritized understanding who they were and their own capacity to flourish. Tom truly believed that within each individual in this community was the wherewithal to lift themselves up to emerge at a higher level due to their own internal resources—it was his job to make them cognizant of that fact.

Another story that echoes the importance of compassionate understanding comes from Dr. David Cole, President of the Medical University of South Carolina, who had the following to say during a conversation we were having about first-year medical students.

"What I constantly drive at with medical students [and others], is that in medicine it's about people. And the quicker the student or anyone else in the practice realizes that, the better you will be. I tell the first-year class coming in that if you are not all about people, leave now. The essence, the beauty, the impact of medicine is the understanding that you are serving people and if you have that as your true viewpoint, everything else falls into place. While it is easy to begin to focus on technology, and technology is important, one must understand that what you must be trying to do is serve the individuals who have given you the opportunity to care for them...

"After more than twenty-five years in the profession, I continue to maintain the 'people view,' the mandate I have just described. It is truly to have the opportunity to care. If one loses sight of that mandate, he or she must readjust, reevaluate or redirect. The practice of medicine is a privilege, a privilege to care about individuals and have an impact on their lives."

Dr. Cole is by no means a foreigner to the medical community, and he has an incredible wealth of knowledge about the human body. Yet he stresses that "the essence, the beauty, the impact of medicine," lies in listening to and respecting each individual he serves, no matter the patient's level of knowledge and furthermore, sees it as his responsibility to build a shared understanding between doctor and patient.

It is possible to perform moral acts without being inspired by compassion, and compassion derived from one's own moral code and the fear of "not being able to recognize yourself in the mirror" is all too common. Compassion demonstrates a sincere feeling for another's misfortune. And, the point I would like to make clear is that if our intent is to show compassion because we may feel guilty if we don't, we send the wrong message, and the deed will show itself as insincere. Humble leadership demands that one shows sincere feeling and is committed to being compassionate to all in their circles; this demand requires greater endurance than what can be supplied by fear or guilt. Furthermore, one will be compassionate with more individuals in more diverse circumstances, when it is motivated by love for the other rather than a limited list of what one thinks is true suffering.

As one recognizes the obligation to facilitate the flourishing of another human being, she or he is inspired with a commitment to act to solve problems and alleviate suffering. The compassionate individual is imbued with a sense of purpose on behalf of others and that purpose calls for treating them with kindness, cheerfulness, charity, helpfulness, generosity, and a caring, forgiving spirit. For this spirit to have life-changing impact, one must seek to truly sympathize with others. Following the examples of Tom Nees and Dr. Cole, one must humble oneself with genuine respect for the aggrieved, listen in order to understand and share the burden, and act decisively with wisdom and discernment to aid their fellow man. If, as we discussed, guilt or fear cannot fuel such an intense lifelong commitment to compassion, where do we find this within ourselves? Can compassion in its most impactful form stem from anything less than genuine love for another?

Love

Love's impact is immeasurable and subject to no limitation, i.e. we will never reach the limit of our capacity for love. Do you agree? What or who we love tells the world who we are! As the recipient of our time, attention, and resources, it often defines our core nature. While for many, love solely conveys the feeling of a deep romantic attraction to someone else, its meaning is not limited to romanticism alone. If we see that it describes a wider range of human experience, namely an intense feeling of deep affection for anyone, anything, any hobby or interest, we will not fear romantic connotations. I do not broaden the meaning of love with any intention of diminishing its intensity; to love is not the same as to like. Love is a feeling that inspires action and in its purest form, is truly infinite and unchangeable. I naturally gravitate to a specific description of love known as *agape* spoken about by the ancient Greeks. By definition, agape love is a committed desire for another's best, their highest good, their flourishing, and is independent of and unconstrained by their behavior. This high love perfects one's love for their neighbor, their friend, their children, their spouse, and the passerby on the street; it is universal. It is a love that does not expect anything in return and is always "others focused." What better accompaniment can there be to make the humble leader more complete. An easily recognized example of unconditional love is found in the following story about a man, his dog, and his best friend.

> The man was wondering who loved him most, the dog or his best friend. To that end, he places the two of them in the trunk of his car and drives across rough roads for a few hours. At the end of the trip, he opens the trunk. Without giving you the answer, I ask, who do you think is happiest to see the man? The moral of this story is may I be the man my dog thinks I am!

You may snicker at our seemingly extreme example of unconditional love and wonder why love is so critical for the humble leader. Loving someone selflessly naturally parallels good leadership.

1. Loving someone means you act for their good in the small moments; these often happen subconsciously or naturally. We choose to see their best qualities, appreciate them for who they are, and be supportive of them. Humble leadership parallels this by definition; we will desire the follower to do well and while some positive moments may demand intentional choices of us, others will naturally flow out of genuine humble states.

2. Loving someone means you recognize your need for them. Humble leaders similarly recognize their need for those who follow them; they appreciate the unique abilities of those they lead and what they bring to the relationship. We do not only need followers. The humble leader is also captivated by worthy individuals who may "outrank" them in one way or another. There is not only a deep respect for what such worthy individuals have undergone and accomplished, but for how they continue to employ their gifts to lift others up—how they lead. The humble leader will seek out such individuals who will be great sources of inspiration and whom they will want to champion as fellow leaders.

3. Loving someone can be a rush as well as a drain. To be sure, there are leaders that are excited to work with those they lead—it is its own high. And, like loving someone, there will be low moments. The intensity of these highs and lows occasionally yield a feeling of crashing and burning. These emotions need not define a loving relationship, nor the relationships of the humble leader.

4. Loving someone can be an uphill battle and similarly, leading others humbly can be a constant challenge. The leader is constantly changing as is the follower, and one must be committed to serving the other as the needs of each change throughout the years.

Humility

Humility can be difficult to define. While most of us know what it is when we see it, we simply tend to string a lot of emotional or touchy-feely words together when asked to tell someone what it means. Further complicating the matter, is the abundance of fool's gold or false humility in our society. With tongue in cheek, I heard a person say this morning, "Humility cries out for recognition." Or the similar phrase, "I am humble and proud of it!" Too often I sense those who claim humility do so with a "touch of pride." I also have a similar feeling when someone claims to be a "servant leader" with an air of pride, as though he or she can now check another accomplishment box. Humility is not a box to be checked, and it is not a skill taught by a class or a book for that matter. True humility can only flourish on a continuum, where each small daily act of humility changes us entirely, deepening its meaning and worth to the individual. It must be transformative in its slow, minute-by-minute increments. Rick Warren described it well in his book: *The Purpose Driven Life: What on Earth Am I Here For?* when he wrote, "Humility is not thinking less of yourself; it is thinking of yourself less."[46]

As citizens of a relatively self-centered society, being surrounded by colleagues who often ask, "What's in it for me?" it can be difficult keeping the interests of others first. Focusing on the flourishing of fellow men and women seems to lose its glow when others' focus seems to be on "self." Susman's findings speak to this very fact when they detail the American cultural shift from a producing to a consuming society.[47] I believe there is a parallel, all too connected shift from a focus on good character traits and virtues to a focus on self and material possessions, which gave rise to the largely socially accepted egocentric person.

I vaguely remember a story told by Tim Keller that took place shortly after he moved to New York. Apparently, Keller was reading *The Village Voice*, an American news and culture paper, known for being the country's first

---

46. Warren, Rick. *Cultivating Community. The Purpose Driven Life: What on Earth Am I Here For?* Grand Rapids. Zondervan, 2002. Page 148.
47. Susman, Warren. *Culture and Commitment, 1929-1945.* G. Braziller, 1973.

alternative newsweekly. As he told the story, a writer by the name of Cynthia Heimel, writing for the *Voice* in the '80s, knew a number of the "to be" stars who, during those years, worked as bouncers in nightclubs, behind the cosmetic counters at Macy's, or at similar part-time jobs that would provide enough income to make ends meet. While they eventually became famous movie stars, they became more unhappy than they were before. In her column, Heimel said that the giant thing they were striving for, the "fame thing" that promised to make everything great, the "success" that would surely make their lives bearable and provide them with the personal fulfillment and happiness they desired actually happened! And yet, nothing truly changed. They were still themselves. The disillusionment of stardom turned many of them into howling and insufferable individuals. With this little story in mind, we should recognize that true joy cannot prevail when one achieves personal, selfish or self-centered goals. Striving after fame, success, and riches does not lay the groundwork for joy and thus the two must not be conflated. The egocentric individual has an excessive focus on that which is temporal in nature and when such is the case, there is never enough. The first boat requires there to be a larger boat; the first car demands a new, more luxurious car; the first home points out that the next home must be bigger and in a "better" neighborhood. Without question, this attitude initiates a self perpetuating wave of never-ending desire for more! To be sure, much of this behavior is related to one's early life and the culture in which they live, and a major catalyst for these desires might be keeping up with the "Joneses!" We are also highly influenced by constant exposure to product and service advertisements, all too-frequent "advice" from social media, and many of today's popular speakers who solely encourage us to pursue higher levels of personal achievement and performance. Think about it! How many songs center on themes of "you can do it" and "pursue your dreams"? Imagine the impact these songs—pride-laced as they are—would instead have if they infused these themes with an expressed desire to serve your fellow man rather than simply seeking one's own "best life." I have absolutely no quarrel with humble high achievers. Without question, I hold that satisfaction with a job well done is important. But should this be our highest good? And will these desires for self-fulfillment not compete with the sacrifices demanded by serving others? The achievement that I so often hear encouraged is solely personal and frequently sought at the expense of others. Pride flourishes in our society today, and we must be wary in our pursuit of our ambition, the roads we believe we must travel or the responsibilities we must carry—what do we sacrifice towards these ends? I believe all too rarely these pursuits will be for the sake of others; pride and its selfish ends will have wormed its way into our hearts, and this must not be tolerated.

I consider humility to be the foundation of all virtues—the whole moral life. It is necessary for the acquisition of all other, highly desirable traits. Consider: How does your purpose fuel your humility, and how can we infuse our society with humility?

I believe that faith, hope, compassion, love, and humility are all connected and must be present simultaneously. Unlike other forms of leadership that tend to follow a well-established paradigm and to check off behavior boxes, the humble leader must recognize the entwined complexity of these five virtues to live them out effectively and synchronously. Through the gentle encouragement and selfless example of the humble leader, faith, which may at first appear to your followers to be of little worth and portend uncertain outcome, can become intrinsic to your follower's way of life and in turn lead to the unmitigated success of one's institution. It is the humble leader whose goal is the flourishing of the individuals in their spheres that will recognize that hope is of vital importance, but only hope invested in worthwhile, life-giving aims; they will thus make daily concerted efforts to inspire realistic hopes that will grow their followers and go the extra mile to make sure that those hopes are proven well-founded. that pays dividends when accepted reasonable and true possibilities. Deep-seated humility will not allow us to fall into the trap of merely pitying others and will rather sustain long-term, genuine compassion that will melt the hard hearted and difficult personalities. And who other than the humble leader will be so fervent and persistent in their love of their fellow man and woman to compassionately sympathize with them, while bolstering their faith and hope? As you may have ascertained already, the humble leader has quite the weight on his shoulders; he or she must be a devoted life-long student of these five virtues and have the goal of becoming an expert. Consider how these rare, but impactful virtues have affected your own life, continue your research, and seek out mentors who display these five virtues with vivacity and grace. In the next section, we will study wisdom and discernment so we will understand what is required to employ these virtues with intention in a variety of situations.

APPLICATION QUESTIONS

Faith

- Explain faith as you understand it, how it compares to other thoughts and beliefs we may entertain, and its value for leaders and followers.

Hope

- How may one establish hopeful and yet realistic expectations for oneself and their followers, and why is that important?

Compassion

- Why is pity fruitless, and will the humble leader be successful in helping others if he/she compares their achievements to others?

- Read through the book of Job. Have you pitied or been pitied in a similar fashion?

- What are realistic ways you can help someone who sees themself as a perpetual victim?

Love

- In an institutional setting, love may be difficult to discuss. Why is this the case and knowing the importance of "love for mankind," how may this difficulty be overcome?

Humility

- How may you develop yourself as a Humble Leader and what aspects of our culture, institutions, and communities fight that aim?

- How are the other four virtues in this section foundational or interwoven with humility?

CHAPTER 5: From Knowing to Understanding to Application: *Wisdom and Judgement*

Wisdom

Wisdom was acknowledged by early Greek philosophers as one of man's most desirable traits. Why do you think the Greeks would say that and is that still true today? We tend to desire faculties adept in handling the practical aspects of life, and we value aptitude in very specific spheres of knowledge; this desire is undoubtedly instilled and fostered by our current education model, but wisdom transcends this. It is not merely the pursuit of an academic degree nor merely the addition of intuition, foresight, or predictive capabilities. While these are important elements of wisdom, a continued interdigitation of life experiences must be thoughtfully considered in light of and with the aim of fostering what is good, true and beautiful, and remembered each day as we plan to act for tomorrow. How does the wise individual present? They listen well, gather vast quantities of information, which their reason integrates piece by piece into a whole; this also allows them to transfer knowledge seamlessly between a variety of experiences and fields. They are slow to react and may recognize that inaction or wordless listening is better suited to a situation. They are extremely respectful and tolerant of others and their issues, and they do not have to be in the limelight. They are self-reflective and imaginative, and thus have access to deeper implications. They are thoughtful in all that they say or do, and their thinking is aware of the impact an idea will have on a community at large.

Does the manifold of experiences of your life synthesize into a single worldview or philosophy that encourages the pursuit of new experiences and wisdom, while also giving you peace, hope, and fortitude through whatever life may bring? In my view, wisdom must have at its base a realization of the transcendentals—everything must be measured against whether or not it is good, true, and beautiful. It is written in the Holy Bible (1 Kings 3:5-12)[48] that God said to Solomon when he became king of Israel: "Ask! What shall I give you?" Solomon's answer was based on his recognition that true wealth is found in wisdom, and "wisdom" was his answer. Solomon became the wisest king on earth and as a result was rewarded later with great wealth and stature.

Wisdom is characteristic of someone who is very observant of life and sees deeply into situations around them. The humble leader seeks out the true nature of things and gains wisdom—a part of that wisdom is knowing "a tomato is a fruit and yet not to put it into a fruit salad." Or in other words, the proper time and place for the usage or disclosure of information is often just as critical. I would like to be able to tell you how to gain such insight, but I know of no rules that get one to that point. What I do know, however, is that we must steep ourselves in the breadth and depth of the world and not observe life as "a parade" to be observed, but become involved as an active participant—what truths are reflected in the world around us and how are we and others around us responding to these truths? Am I or someone I lead in discordance with the true nature of the world around us? We must seek to truly understand others, explore other cultures, listen to their stories with intention and ask questions, and courageously challenge others with the desire to know how things truly are.

Occasionally, when you seek to understand another or be understood, phrases such as "walking a mile in another's shoes," "seeing through another's eyes" or "living in another's skin" may come to mind. Since none of these are possible in the most real sense, the best thing one can do is to take a genuine interest in others and their concerns, which is more than just sensing their feelings and emotions. To use a sports metaphor, one can

---

48. 1 Kings 3:5, NKJV.

enjoy a football game by sitting in the stadium with other fans and experience the emotional enthusiasm for the "home team." Even better, one can sit on the bench with team members and feel the intensity of the challenge as they come off or go on the field of play. Better yet, get in the game and experience first-hand the thrill of running, blocking, tackling, or catching a pass. This is what it means to take a genuine interest in anything and show concern for all that takes place. Daniel Goleman, in his book, *Emotional Intelligence*, emphasizes understanding others as the first element of empathy, a bond between individuals who can relate to and share their challenges and opportunities.[49]

Having grown up in a small, rural community, I didn't find understanding the perspective of your neighbor to be much of a challenge. The culture seemed simple, and most people exhibited similar behavior. It is frequently said that if you never leave "hometown," you run the risk of seeing the whole world as "hometown." Of course, this is a very simple metaphor—there is nothing wrong with cherishing one's roots, and there are many ways to see the world—books, movies, lectures—all of which help us avoid the myopia that plagues many of us. It is important, however, that we make the effort to learn of what's going on beyond our typical spheres of influence because this knowledge is a great contributor to wisdom. The greatest thinkers of all time have thought about wisdom , talked about it and written about in some of our greatest books. Make use of literature. It will serve you well! It is worth mentioning because many do not take advantage of these opportunities and live an entire life utterly lacking in continued self-education. It wasn't until I left home that I really began noticing how differently some people behaved. This difference became most obvious when I was conducting a leadership workshop for faculty at one of the Schools in the University of Maryland Baltimore Campus. During this particular session we were focused on values. After a brief, general discussion of values, I asked the question, "What values do you hold that are non-negotiable?" Considering the question to be somewhat rhetorical and simply hoping to initiate discussion, I was a bit surprised when one of

---

49. Goleman, Daniel. *Emotional Intelligence: Why It Can Matter More Than IQ.* New York: Bantam Books, 1995. Print.

the participants stated that in his country all values are negotiable. While his answer initiated a brief debate, it left me with a new awareness of cultural differences and the need for humble leaders to explore them carefully. Short of living in a culture different from one's own, being a part of a multicultural society that is commonplace today, a study of psychosocial and sociopolitical literature relevant to a given culture can be extremely useful. A study of this nature provides a knowledge base on which one can build the courage necessary to participate in productive conversations and ask informed, non-judgemental questions that show genuine interest.

How does one listen with intention? We cannot listen simply for the sake of being entertained or gaining information; we must desire for what we hear to be a catalyst for action—how does this inspire us to act? Intentional listening thus surpasses so-called "active listening," which is merely an addition of head nods and eye contact. If the person speaking can see that you are listening with the intention to act on what they say, they too will be encouraged and inspired. Intentional listening can be seen in thoughtful responses and will be foundational to building mutually desirable relationships. While intentional listening may only bridge the gap between two understandings so far and we may never know exactly "how things are" for another, it is a worthy pursuit and is a great aid in building unity between individuals.

When we listen with the intention of being changed by what we learn and compelled to act, we become fervent pursuers of truth. Our pride in our own understanding has to become dwarfed before the perspective of the person we are speaking with and the value they bring to the conversation. The humble leader will courageously ask questions with grace that seek to get at the true heart of the issue and will inspire his or her listeners to do the same. When common ground is not reached that may signal a need for outside research and input before reconvening discussion, I champion you to be the bulwark that holds the door open for discussing the matter at a later date. An important and hopefully obvious point here is that the humble leader is not debating to win, make themselves heard, get their two-sense in, or undermine others—the goal is that truth is said, understood and can be acted upon.

I grew up in the Welcome Community, a small locale that is three miles from downtown Greenville, SC. My first twelve years of formal education took place at Welcome Elementary, Junior and High School. I attended Welcome Baptist Church. My first and only real part-time job was at Community Drug Store, just over one mile from my parent's home. As I look back, I was a little like the frog in the children's story about a *The Frog in the Well*—anyone trying to tell me that there really was life away from "home" was not to be believed.[50] Even though I completed my first college experience in Charleston, SC, it did not occur to me that my future would take me and my family to places other than Greenville, and I had no interest in leaving. When I broached this subject with my Dad, a common laborer, terrific parent, and wonderful gentleman with only a sixth-grade education, he simply stated, "If you want to make a contribution to the world based on who you are and who you want to be, you must leave home." During the thirty years following this conversation, I had the privilege of working for and influencing the efforts of a company that did business in more than one hundred and sixty countries around the world and myself spent time in Scandinavia, England, Europe, the Middle East, Asia, South America, and Australia. While I do not consider myself a "wise person," this travel afforded me a wealth of opportunities to develop more of that virtue than would have been the case had I remained in hometown. Thanks, Dad!

Practical wisdom, as John Bradshaw wrote in his book, *Reclaiming Virtue*, "is the ability to do the right thing, at the right time, for the right reason,"[51] and always invites a long term perspective. The wise individual knows that a strength used to excess is a weakness and if underutilized, is also a weakness. For example, if one's strength is initiating, a "let's get started" kind of person, too much application of the strength by a given individual will define him or her as hyperactive or too insistent. On the other hand, when this strength is underutilized, he or she may be seen as passive or too laid back. Furthermore, wisdom is a habit of performing an action with the highest degree of moral acceptability under any given circumstance—one

50. Tsai, Irene Y., Caprio, Pattie, Joyce, Lin. *The Frog In The Well.* Philadelphia, CE Bilingual Books LLC. 2008.

51. Bradshaw, John. *Reclaiming Virtue: How We Can Develop the Moral Intelligence to Do the Right Thing at the Right Time for the Right Reason.* New York. Random House USA, Inc. 29 April 2009.

that avoids wrongdoing. As you pursue a greater awareness and understanding of how the world works in fundamental ways, you will exercise more self-control, become more alert and careful, and become more flexible. Pursuing wisdom will put you in a class of leaders who are humble, embrace wonder, are truly open to new ideas, and life-giving.

Judgement

Decision-making and judgement give rise to one of the most common complaints I have heard from employees, "The boss will not make a decision and that leaves all of us 'hanging in the wind!'" A close second complaint is, "The boss decides on a given direction this morning and changes his mind before the day ends." Frustration prevails and precious, irreplaceable time is wasted. Decision-making is a conscious intellectual activity. It calls for acquiring knowledge of the issue through review of appropriate literature and research, interviewing individuals involved, and an assessment of the long-term impact in comparison with alternative options. It also often entails sympathetic and tolerant discussions when other people are involved. This allows the leader to establish a well informed belief or course of action based on said beliefs, and then requires one to establish procedures that must be put in place to carry out the decision. In the end, a choice is made.

The leader who is willing to take the time and invest the effort to implement such a process for decision-making will serve his or her institution well. Here are some bullet points to make note of:

1. Recognize problems and initiate a process to prepare a response; be proactive when the situation demands action.

2. Systematically gather information, including input from others, carefully sort through the complex findings, and make sure to address the root cause of issues.

3. Be cognizant of others and foster opportunities for them. Use consensus when possible and appropriate.

4. Formulate decisions that are systematic and would be replicable by others. Nevertheless, do not be afraid to make difficult decisions and pursue your convictions without fear of disgruntled reactions. Either way, you are accountable for every decision you make.

5. Communicate your decisions in a clear and timely fashion and make sure that they are pragmatic and executable in a like manner.

As I have warned before, beware of biases when making decisions. Much of our intellectual activity: our thinking, our reason, and our memory are inclined to show prejudices against someone or something. Cognitive biases are easy to come by, and it is easy to make a habit of including them in our decision-making process. First of all, recognize that there are numerous forms of bias and that they do come into play when one is making a decision. One that I hear most frequently is "confirmation bias," which is the tendency to interpret certain "new" evidence as confirmation of one's existing beliefs. Another I hear almost as frequently is "social bias," which occurs when we give preference to certain people or groups for no justifiable reason e.g., one makes a decision to favor someone, a friend or favorite employee. It is essential that you avoid the tendency to take the easy way out by deciding to please a single individual or group.

You have often heard parents say to a youngster, "You don't have to learn everything the hard way! I have been there, so listen." In most cases this is true and good advice for the younger person when it comes to decision-making. Parents' advice is usually based on extensive experience and will be of high value to the girl or boy trying to learn a few of "life's ropes." If the younger person is prone to take advice at all, he or she will yield to the authority with a positive response and few if any questions. This elicits a favorable response from Mom or Dad but may well be the beginning of a habit that doesn't serve one well in the workplace. I highly recommend caution for parents who may be tempted to use this tack beyond the home. One should not lead on the job the way they lead at home, and expect childlike obedience—the adults who follow you are more sensitive to your biases.

Keep in mind that decisions often impact numerous people and that "perfect" decisions are difficult to come by. While in retrospect one will usually find that a little "tweaking" could have been done before moving forward, keep this to a minimum by those you are leading beforehand. It is at this time, when the "imperfect" decision has been made, that humble leadership is of its greatest value because followers of this person are not inept! They have been a part of the process all along and stand ready to "fill the gap" when necessary. If for no other reason, their respect for the "boss" will always make him or her look good.

APPLICATION QUESTIONS

Wisdom

- Are you a wise person? If your answer is yes, how did you become that person and what evidence will I see in your behavior that convinces me that you are wise?

- How may one place proper value on "hometown experiences," yet develop a valued appreciation for experiences of others that were developed in a different culture?

- It is stated above that wisdom is a habit of performing an action with the highest degree of moral acceptability under any given circumstance. If that statement describes you, how may I learn to behave similarly?

- How can you and your followers develop the habit of considering decisions in light of what is good, true and beautiful?

Judgement

- Describe how you would teach your followers to deal with "confirmation bias."

- How may you lead so that your style is not like that which often describes the parent—do it my way?

CHAPTER 6: Your Source of Self-Respect:
Respect and Responsibility

As human beings, we are born with individual sovereignty. Empowered with self-determination, we have the ability to govern ourselves to make honest and peaceful choices without any interference from outside sources or bodies. Fortunately, we live in a sovereign country where this ability—and many say, *right*—is honored. In fact, our right to self-determination is a cardinal principle in modern international law. Individual sovereignty, *self-determination*, are not mere phrases; they are imperative principles of action. I cannot make the importance of this clearer. As you give thought to self-determination as an imperative principle, I ask that you reflect on the level of personal responsibility that one must engender, employ, and accordingly, make a part of everyday life to justify our having this birthright. When we begin to acknowledge the full ream of our responsibilities as a part of our way of life, it becomes a duty to act or choose a course of action to which we are morally and legally bound. As an example, automobile accidents due to mechanical failure are uncommon. In most instances, these accidents are due to willful and unnecessary self-distraction– failure of someone to take full, personal responsibility for the power of their actions.

The different levels of responsibility that a community feels towards its members can have alarming effects. David Brooks tells us a story about Jane Jacobs, who was looking out her second-story window at her Greenwich Village street below when she saw what appeared to be a possible kidnapping.[52] As she was preparing to go downstairs to intervene, she noticed that people were coming from various locations and surrounded the man. While the event was not what Jacobs first thought, I'm sure that the fact that the community was coming together gave comfort to the residents. This experience was in sharp contrast to that of the events on March 13, 1964, when a New York woman (Kitty Genovese) was killed while witnesses did nothing.[53] It appears as though Ms. Jacobs felt the need to take an active role in her "protective community" when the need arose, while those in Ms. Genovese's building felt otherwise.

I have diligently studied my nature, submitted myself to the assessment of many others, and to a certain degree, I am confident that I know who I am. Additionally, I have known since my earliest years of awareness that no two people are alike, and therefore I must respect the priorities and values of others and recognize how my decisions will inevitably affect the world around me. For these and other reasons, I have assumed total responsibility for my life and the impact it has on others. For example, if someone happens to be angry, I ask myself if I played a role in that anger? If someone fails to reach a specific goal, did I fail to provide the right support at the appropriate time? If someone is sad, is it my fault? Obviously, this kind of thinking can be taken too far and become unhealthy. However, experience over the years has proven to me that thinking of others first is a good idea.

As we accept personal responsibility for our own actions and conduct, it is natural that we dignify the imperative of respect for other persons and things with the same level of importance. Respect and responsibility are best understood in tandem. Wisdom is understanding how my responsibilities towards myself and others are fueled and defined by my respect for them. For example, the respect owed to the sanctity of all human life

---

52. Brooks, David. The States of Community Building 1, *The Second Mountain: The Quest for a Moral Life*. New York, Random House, 2019, Page 265.

53. Gansberg, Martin. "'37 Who Saw Murder Didn't Call the Police' Apathy at Stabbing of Queens Woman Shocks Inspector." *New York Times,* March 27, 1964, Page 1.

This event gave rise to a psychological study referred to the term, *bystander effect,* which refers to the phenomenon in which the greater the number of people present the less people are to help a person in distress.

entails certain responsibilities towards the rest of the human race. Or stated another way, my respect for another's sovereignty may help me draw the line between what is my responsibility and what is theirs. How do you see respect and responsibility playing out in your day-to-day interactions with others?

Responsibility lays the groundwork for so many other traits common to the humble leader, especially respect. It is a quality that, by intent, develops over time, and enables you to be the best version of the person you are intended to be. While the decision to become responsible or more responsible may introduce quite a challenge in one's life, achieving that endpoint is certainly possible. The first step is to accept how much depends solely on you—your thoughts, perceptions, actions, and spoken words. As responsibility becomes more integral to your way of life, respect for all that is around you follows and the more you show respect, the more respect is shown to you. Thus, there begins a self-perpetuating wave that serves you and your followers exceptionally well.

Respect plays out as a form of fairness, decency, or grace that is shared between individuals or individuals and a society; it creates a bond based on admiration, appreciation, or fondness that is independent of time and distance. Meaning, if our relationship is built on mutual and deep-seated respect, we may enjoy each other's company today, part ways for a period, and yet pick up where we left off without "missing a beat." Respect is of critical importance, especially in today's society as it allows for agreeable disagreements and encourages continued advancement.

There is a sign at the entrance of the Arlington National Cemetery that reads: "Silence and Respect." I was speaking with one of the Navy's enlisted persons a few weeks ago who served as a member of the U.S. Navy Ceremonial Guard in Washington, DC. As he described his training and the nature of his assignment at the Arlington National Cemetery, I asked, "What do you remember most about your training?" His answer was, "It's not about you!" He elaborated saying: "They firmly implanted in our minds that the individual being honored had made the supreme sacrifice. The honoree, his family, loved ones, and friends deserve the highest respect.

It was about them, not us!" For the humble leader, it is always about others, not us. Whether it is the loss of life, failure to pass an examination, a child's illness or that of a friend, one's sincere, compassionate recognition and understanding of the dilemmas they are facing is always encouraging to the person experiencing the stress of life's challenges. The humble leader can demonstrate the "not about me" attitude simply by listening, and this "silence and respect" is clear evidence of his or her taking full, personal responsibility.

A few years ago, I held the Director of Marketing position at The Upjohn Company. At that time, I was relatively young and inexperienced but had a well-developed "not always right but never in doubt attitude." A few marketing colleagues and I had come up with an aggressive, well-studied plan that would move the company up in market share in a category where we were currently lagging. We were convinced of our future success and my responsibility was to sell the idea to my boss and through him, sell it to his boss, the company's president. To that end, I arranged a meeting with him and made our case.

My boss was Reed Peterson. Reed grew up in a Mormon household in Ogdon, Utah. He had many of the respectful, service-oriented traits that seem to be common to people with that background. I presented our proposed plan, he listened very carefully, asked good questions, and after an hour or so in conversation, agreed with the plan and promised to carry it forward. Unfortunately, a couple of weeks passed without me hearing anything from him! Since my "team" was pushing from their end and I was getting nothing from above, serious frustration began to emerge.

Reed's behavior toward me was always respectful and encouraging. While our routine was to meet once each Monday at 11:00 a.m. in his office to keep each other "up to speed," he was inclined to come to my office between those regular meetings, especially if something important came up. In almost every case, he would give me a call with the question, "Do you have a minute?" I would answer yes and within ten minutes, he would walk through the door.

It was on a Wednesday morning when I got that call. As usual, he did not explain why he wanted to come down, so I assumed it had to do with the plan. I also assumed his reply was going to be negative since I had heard nothing in over two weeks. I had ten minutes to redevelop my argument.

As he came in, he walked to the windows, looking out as if trying to decide what to say and how to say it, and I decided to make it easy for him. I said, "What's the verdict?"

He said, "Verdict?"

I said, "The plan, of course? Are we going forward?"

He said, "The decision has not been made yet." With that, I exploded. When I finally took a breath, he said, "If you are finished, I would like to tell you why I'm here."

After a very feeble attempt to apologize, I asked, "What's up?"

He said, "I'm sorry for not getting to you with an answer earlier but I haven't been feeling well for the past few weeks and was diagnosed on Monday with Stage IV prostate cancer. I came down this morning because I just wanted you to know and ask for your prayers!"

That, my friends, was the first and only high-energy lesson I had and would ever need to understand the value of respect! I was so intent on making my point, which included an appropriate criticism of the boss, I failed to read the prevailing atmosphere—facial expressions, slowness of movement as he walked across the floor in my office, hands in his pockets, tone of voice, unspoken words—all of which made up a message I'd completely missed. Reed passed away a few short months later. The memory of that experience will last forever, and here is what has lingered over the years. As a sovereign individual, I had within my being the "authority" to choose a course of action. Based on my personal responsibility for others and the concomitant respect, I should have chosen a different course of action. I did not.

There are numerous approaches to defining the term "respect." At the beginning of this section I stated that respect is a form of fairness, decency, or grace that is shared between individuals or individuals and a society. Respect naturally grows out of esteem for shared character and deep moral values. We can have a respect for transient and tangible values—someone's money, rank, fame, even their achievements—but it is never as lasting and impactful as that intangible respect and deep appreciation that inexplicably appears every time a close friend or mentor whom we have shared life and its beautiful intricacies and challenges with walks through the door.

I once heard it said: "Don't judge my choices without understanding my reasons." Somewhere along the way, I learned that people do things for their own reasons—sometimes they are for good, sometimes not. It may be well, then, to respect others and make an effort to learn of their reasons.

The humble leader has a sincere feeling of admiration and deference toward others and their ideas. As mentioned earlier, Collins suggested in *Good to Great,* the humble leader looks in the mirror after something has gone wrong and takes the blame for failing to provide appropriate leadership. On the other hand, when things have gone right, he or she looks out the window to the people and gives them credit for successfully taking advantage of the opportunity to reach the desired results. John Maxwell refers to this as the "Mirror Principle," stating: "The first person we must examine is ourselves."

I was frequently told to respect others when I was still a very small child: respect your parents, respect your elders, respect the police, etc. At that young age, I didn't know the definition of the term, but I knew how to demonstrate it based on observation of family and friends who showed respect to others. As time went on, I added to my understanding by enjoying the benefits of respect and learning the disadvantages of disrespect. I share the following story from my first job with you because it was the first time I really understood the true meaning and value of the virtue and experienced the emotional satisfaction from being shown respect. My understanding had finally developed beyond the "command" to respect others and the mere dictionary definition.

My first "real" job as a young boy—around thirteen years of age—was that of a "soda jerk" at Community Drug Store in Greenville, South Carolina. I was a little too young to be "formally" employed but my older brother was a friend of the owners, and they decided to take the chance and counted on my reaching legal age before anyone knew the whole story. Community Drug, as we called it, was located on Easley Bridge Road, less than three miles from downtown, and around twelve miles from downtown Easley, South Carolina. Easley Bridge Road was a busy thoroughfare. For this, lack of close-by competition and a few other reasons, the store did a fairly brisk business. The store was owned by the Westmorelands and Lawhorns. Bill Westmoreland was a pharmacist and Ed Lawhorn, formerly a Navy corpsman was an assistant pharmacist—a professional position no longer in existence. Bill passed away shortly before I went to work, so Ed was the boss.

At the young age of thirteen, it is likely that I approached the job as did others of the same age—not too crazy about having to "work" but liked to get a few bucks at the end of the week. As I recall, I didn't see myself as being of much value as an employee. I was grossly overweight—my nickname to some was Double Dip. I was not a good student in school. I was not an athlete. And, while the fifth of six children of two of the world's most loving parents, I didn't feel I had much to offer the world in which I found myself. After having taken some sort of "psychological test" in school and found to be best suited for cleaning test tubes in a laboratory, I was pretty sure my self-assessment was correct.

It was just under two years after going to work at the store when Ed decided to remodel. His intent was to change the layout, install new shelving and display cases, replace the old fountain with a new one and add a low bar with stools. Everyone was excited—employees and customers—and I was going along for the ride. By the way, I was a pretty good employee… went to work on time (most of the time) respected the customers and performed most duties willingly.

After a few weeks, much of the "heavy lifting" for the remodeling project was completed, and it was time for painting and final clean-up. Ed had picked up color swatches from the paint store and was debating which colors would go where. To my utter surprise, he called me (I was then known as Shorty to Ed, not Double Dip) to the back of the store where he had the swatches laid out. After explaining his opinion relative to the need for new paint, he asked me to recommend colors for the various locations. I studied the options carefully, asked for a little time to think it over, then gave my suggestions. You guessed it. Ed took all my recommendations, and I had the pleasure of viewing the paint colors on those walls long after I had become a pharmacist—another part of the story.

Ed had encouraged now deceased Ralph Wilkie—a young man from a relatively poor family whose dad had passed while he was quite young—to attend the School of Pharmacy at the Medical University of South Carolina (MUSC). Ralph was a good student in high school, became a part of the student body at MUSC, and, upon completion of all requirements, joined Ed as a pharmacist. (Ralph's presence was important to Ed, since Ed was an assistant pharmacist and was not permitted by law to run the store without a pharmacist on duty). While this was never discussed, I am convinced that due to Ralph's success and the change Ed had seen in me over the years, he felt comfortable encouraging me to follow Ralph's path. He did so and offered me the opportunity to work at the store when home for school breaks, including summer recesses.

As I said earlier, I was not a good student during my early years of elementary, junior and high school. With my academic performance over all those years, I did not expect to be accepted at the School of Pharmacy. As luck would have it, though, I had taken numerous science classes in high school and did very well in each case. On the strength of performance in the sciences, I was accepted and joined the class of 1960 in September 1956.

Ed continued to follow my academic career with serious interest and encouragement. For example, he learned during my trip home for Thanksgiving holidays—I had just begun my second year—that I had taken an after-school job in a Charleston Drug Store to help with expenses. He asked: "How do you plan to get to work?" Now, that question alone was a demonstration of the sense of responsibility he felt towards me, even just as one of his employees. He knew my family well, had a good idea of my financial status and was not surprised when I answered: "I'm looking around for something I can afford—possibly a motorbike."

Again, acting on the responsibility he felt he had to shield me from danger, he said: "Motorbikes aren't safe!" and that ended the conversation. Before I returned to school after the holiday, Ed presented me with a second-hand Buick in pristine condition—no strings attached. He told me the car was mine to keep and to trade it for something of my choice upon graduation.

While MUSC graded on the A, B, C, F scoring scale, by today's GPA standard, I graduated with the equivalent of 3.8 out of a possible 4.0. My score on the S. C. State Board of Examiners for Licensure was above 95% out of a possible 100. This may sound boastful and, in one sense it is. However, I share it with you because it clearly demonstrates the value of the "Ed Lawhorns" of our world who recognize the need to respect others, knowing that respect initiates a self-perpetuating wave of encouragement so valuable to our youth. While I had made little contribution to society at this stage in my life, Ed saw my unseen potential, placed high value on what I could achieve, and provided the encouraging base on which I would build throughout the years ahead. Were it not for people of that ilk; I would not be writing to you today! Ed Lawhorn was a most humble, respectful man. I have enjoyed great benefits from following his path.

During the mid-1100s, Barnard of Chartres[54] coined the well-known metaphor, *standing on the shoulders of giants,* by comparing John of Salisbury[55] to dwarfs perched on the shoulders of giants. Salisbury, who described himself as John the Little, explained that the people of his ilk could see more and farther than their predecessors, not because they had keener vision or greater height, but because they were lifted up and borne aloft on their giant's towering stature. To many, the metaphor, which expresses the meaning of "discovering truth by building on previous discoveries," be-

---

54. Barnard of Chartres (France) was a twelfth-century French Neo-Platonist philosopher, scholar, and administrator.

55. John of Salisbury, born in Salisbury, England, was an English author, philosopher, educationalist diplomat and bishop of the Roman Catholic Diocese of Chartres (France).

came a familiar expression in English when Isaac Newton stated, "If I have seen further it is by standing on the shoulders of Giants."[56]

I have heard Barnard's metaphor, also known as the *metaphor of dwarfs,* used many times over the years to communicate respect for the valued contribution of others to one's level of achievement. I have used that metaphor for similar reasons and to encourage our younger, less experienced population to respect others. However, I have never used nor heard it used in a way more personal and grateful than I did a few days ago.

Earlier this week (5 February 2019) I attended the Annual Induction Ceremony for the local chapter of the National Academy of Inventors[57] at the Medical University of South Carolina. One of MUSC's inductees and keynote speakers for the event was Michael J. Yost, Ph. D.[58]

As I listened to his comments, I thought it would be useful to share some of his thoughts with you.

Mike began with a statement that he said was used frequently by those engaged in surgery: "We stand on the shoulders of giants." He continued with a story about vacationing with his family as a young boy. "We would crowd into Dad's car, drive to southeast Ohio, Appalachian country, enjoy picnics with family—aunts, uncles, cousins—and go swimming in the lake. Dad would get in the water, scrunch down so one of us could get on his shoulders and, when the time was right, spring out of the water and let us go. I'm sure many of you can relate to the experience and for me, that was when I began thinking about 'standing on the shoulder of giants!'"

Mike continued to describe that sometime later, he was on a business trip to Washington, DC. He arrived a day early and, along with his ten-year-old son, Erick, met his Dad so they could tour the Aerospace Museum.

56. Sir Isaac Newton was an English mathematician, physicist, astronomer, theologian, and author.
57. The National Academy of Inventors® is a member organization comprising U.S. and international universities, and governmental and non-profit research institutes.
58. Michael J. Yost, Ph. D., Professor and Vice Chairman for the Department of Experimental Surgery, Medical University of South Carolina, Charleston, SC.

They went there because "Dad" wanted Erick to see his projects that were on display. Mike told us that his dad, David J. Yost,[59] was a person who helped America lead the world in science and technology and was the *giant* on whose shoulders Mike stood as he became the man he is today.

Mike moved on to a short discussion of his early years as a graduate student and identified his mentor, Louis Terracio (Lou), Ph. D.[60] He described Lou as a best friend, stating that, "he has been a tremendous help to me throughout my career. He spent many hours with me, day and night, as I was working toward my first 'K25 award,'[61] which was required of me as a young faculty member." At the time, Mike was deeply involved as a student and had a young family and was experiencing all the stress that young men and women do at that state in their career. During one of their mentoring conversations, Lou made the comment, "Mike, some of this stuff you're doing is great, and we need to get it out there. We need for some people to be able to use this stuff. You need to start patenting your work." Mike's retort was, "I don't know how to do all of that. I just want to get through graduate school."

Lou Terracio is a giant on whose shoulders Mike Yost stood! Following Lou's encouragement to get his work patented and into the community at large, Mike phoned a family friend, Jim Fergason,[62] and said, "Jim, I'm struggling. I don't know what to do. I have too many things to do and my mentor is telling me I've got to patent these things." After a little discussion that gave him the "lay of the land," Jim said, "That is good stuff; you ought to patent it. There are people who can help you. So, I want you to quiet

59. David J. Yost was educated at Ohio State Johns Hopkins Universities and worked in the Applied Physics Laboratory at Johns Hopkins University, Baltimore, MD. As an employee in the Laboratory he was engaged in the development of the Apollo astronauts' space suits that were used when walking on the moon; the guidance system for the Pershing 2A Missile, a solid-fueled two-stage ballistic missile; the guidance system for Cruise Missiles, designed to deliver a large warhead over long distances with high precision—the list goes on.

60. Louis Terracio, Ph. D., is Professor and Vice Dean for Research, Basic Science and Craniofacial Biology at New York College of Dentistry, New York, NY.

61. The K25 is a Mentored Quantitative Research Career Development Award, and its purpose is to attract to NIH-relevant research those investigators whose quantitative science and engineering research has thus far not been focused primarily on questions of health and disease.

62. James Lee Fergason, Professor of Chemistry at Kent State University, Kent, OH.

your mind, start trusting your intuition, trust your uncreative thoughts, and get that out there into the world." In addition to being the Yost's family friend, James Lee (Jim) Fergason was an American inventor and business entrepreneur. A member of the National Inventors Hall of Fame, Fergason is best known for his work on an improved liquid crystal display, or the LCD that we see everyday. He held over one hundred U.S. patents at the time of his death. Fergason's shoulders were another set on which Dr. Yost stood as he was becoming the person he is today.

Mike continued to tell us: "Richard M. (Rick) Bell, M. D.,[63] was my first chairman in academia. While with Rick, I worked on a submission for my first 'R grant.'[64] I failed and found myself sitting in the Chairman's *big chair*, directly across from him and his desk. After completing my tale of woe, Rick said, 'Michael, did someone die today because you didn't get the grant?'"

I said, 'No.'

He continued, 'Did someone lose an arm or leg today because you didn't get the grant?'

I said, 'No.'

He said, 'Mike, you're having a good day. Why don't you go back to your lab, try it again and make it better this time!'

We stand on the shoulders of giants! Why? Because they bend down, respect the potential they see, lift us up, and provide needed help along the way."

Giants like Mike's Dad, Jim Fergason, Lou Terracio, and Rick Bell were not born giants, nor did they make their mark alone. They did so by pursuing life with a thoughtful purpose, diligence, integrity, and a focus on

---

63. Richard M, Bell, M. D., Chairman of Surgery, University of South Carolina, Columbia, SC. He was a flight surgeon in the USAF and, along with Brent E. Krantz, M. D. established a worldwide network for trauma and acute care surgery.

64. R Grant is a research grant supporting research by NIH.

the flourishing of others. Those traits are worthy of respect and have served others exceedingly well over the years.

Up to now, we have discussed personal responsibility as a necessary trait for the humble leader because it matures the shoulders on which others may stand; it is the foundation for respect and many other behaviors crucial for humble leadership. This trait is a collection of personal and professional obligations that he or she must accept to reflect accountability for all moral, ethical, and legal behavior considering laws of man and nature. This is a significant assignment and, as I heard it said, if you want to avoid it, an alibi is always handy—don't yield to the temptation!

There are those who argue firmly, listen to your conscience, i.e., if it says don't do it, don't do it! In general, I think listening to one's conscience is a good idea. However, Mark Twain had to deal with the heart vs. conscience in *The Adventures of Huckleberry Finn*. As you may recall, Huck had a few moral conflicts as he struggled with his conscience, and a major problem had to do with the overall influence of society and its values. It seemed that society had twisted him so that his conscience gave him bad advice. Since our space is limited, I will not provide the detail of his challenge but will share this quote: "In a crucial moral emergency a sound heart is a safer guide than an ill-trained conscience."[65]

Remember, the heart is where your greatest loves are. It is where the things in which you hope the most are located! So, how about your heart? Is it where you hold "me first?" Is it where you hold selfishness and unreliability? Or is it where you hold the important value, responsibility?

I mentioned earlier that people do things for their own reasons. Is that true? If someone should ask me to do something and I do it, do I carry out the request for their reason or mine? At first blush, I say I do it for their reason. However, after a little more thought, it is likely I internalized and evaluated the request based on my standards of behavior. If the request

---

65. Twain, Mark. *The Adventures of Huckleberry Finn*. Berkeley, University of California Press, 1988, page 806.

met my standards, I took possession and carried it out as though it were mine. If you find this observation reasonable, then it may shed light on comments such as, "Don't tell me what to do! Don't tell me what to think! I will do it my way!" If the foregoing is close to true, then humble leaders must really get to know their colleagues!

So, how do we develop total responsibility?

The first and, for some, the most difficult step in your professional or personal life is taking ownership of all your mistakes. This ownership includes errors of omission and commission of the past, as well as those that may occur in the future and try to avoid making the same mistakes. Stop trying to justify the wrong endpoint based on the happenings of something or someone else. Stop making promises you know you can't keep. Stop putting it off. Stop complaining. Plan your day and keep your plan. In other words, stop doing things that make you irresponsible and start being more thoughtful and do things that make you more responsible. For example, if you can't keep an appointment, cancel ahead of time. If you tend to "lose your cool," take a tighter control of your emotions. Remember that trust is extremely important and must be earned, and let others know you are willing to work for it. Be consistent, reliable, and self-disciplined.

Father Francis P. Foley, Command Chaplain at the Naval Academy, and I touched base on this topic during our discussion of humble leadership. Following his comments on how he defined the responsibility and comported himself accordingly, I asked how, as an officer and chaplain, was he able to established rapport with those who were expected to follow his lead. His reply was:

> I would always say the same thing to all the chaplains or petty of-ficers when they newly arrived here: "If there's something that you think I'm doing that I shouldn't be, tell me. If there's something that you think I should be doing and am not doing, tell me. If there's something you think we could be doing better or I could be doing better, tell me. Don't ever assume that I know everything, because I don't. I won't promise that I'll always agree with you.

That's not part of the deal and I may not agree. But I will promise to never get upset or use the 'flame spray,' 'How dare you?' or, 'I'm in charge and that's none of your business,' or 'just do as you're told!' I'll never do that. I want there to be an environment where you tell me, especially if there's something that I should be doing that I'm not or there's something I'm doing that I shouldn't be doing, 'Hey, Father, Sir, Chaplain, you shouldn't really be doing that.' Tell me. I need to hear that." I can think of numerous times where, although mostly inconsequential, fortunately, I just missed something. It was at these times when, because of relationships, when another chaplain or one of the petty officers would say, "Hey, sir, I think we need to reach out to this area. We need to get over and visit this unit. You were a little hard on that person. I think it wasn't necessarily your intention, but…" And I've thought, "You're right. Maybe I was a little hard on that person." Even when joking! I can think of one instance where I had joked with somebody and later on somebody came back and said, "They were very sensitive about that, and they'll really stew over your comments." So, I thought, "Okay!" and I went to that person and just brought it in the course of our conversation and I simply said, "Oh, by the way, I think I crossed a line kidding you about this incident, and I apologize." And it made all the difference in the world, almost immediately, in our working relationship. I would never have been aware about how sensitive the person was had my colleague not felt comfortable enough to bring the situation to my attention. So, these are a few small examples and I know that in my life there have been others. Has my approach to rapport and responsibility been effective? I don't know but hope so. Of the people whom I've worked with, particularly at the end of their assignment when they're transferring out, because I always ask them the question: "All right, there are no more fitness reports or no more evaluations. Tell me, what was the good and what was the bad, and if so, what was the ugly? I need to grow and create a better environment. Your answer will help me do just that!"

Obviously, Father Foley's views reflect a high level of maturity and courage common to effective leaders. It also underscores the value of encouraging feedback and honesty from those who follow. I can assure you there will be fewer surprises, and it will be less risky to take responsibility.

Since no one's fate can be separated from the fate of others, responsibility is never limited to the self. Therefore, to what extent do I consider myself responsible for others? In one of his *Devotions upon Emergent Occasions*, John Donne (1573—1631), a metaphysical poet and cleric in the Church of England wrote:

> *No man is an island,*
> *Entire of itself,*
> *Every man is a piece of the continent,*
> *A part of the main.*
> *If a clod be washed away by the sea,*
> *Europe is the less.*
> *As well as if a promontory were.*
> *As well as if a manor of thy friend's*
> *Or of thine own were:*
> *Any man's death diminishes me,*
> *Because I am involved in mankind,*
> *And therefore never send to know for whom the bell tolls;*
> *It tolls for thee.*[66]

While I am very comfortable when alone, i.e., I don't necessarily need to be "in the crowd," membership in the community is important and with this membership comes certain requirements. As a humble leader, give this some thought!

Many of you will remember the story of "David and Goliath."[67] David was in the fields, tending the family's sheep. In David's case, all he would

66. Donne, John. Meditation XVII, *Devotions upon Emergent Occasions*. Church of England, Westminster, 1624.

67. 1 Samuel 17, NLT.

have needed to report was that a lion had appeared, snatched a lamb from the flock, and "How sad, too bad!" David, however, was built of sterner stuff. "I went out after him!" he said. Next came Goliath: nine feet tall, heavily armed, and seemingly unbeatable. David, who had just arrived at the military encampment with food for his brothers and for their captain, heard the giant's cursing challenge and immediately asserted himself: "Who is this Philistine that he should defy the armies of the living God?" (1 Samuel 17:26) Saul and his people were saying, "He's too big to kill!" David was saying, "He's too big to miss!" This is responsibility at its best!

There are many authoritative sources that reflect on the community and the notion that man is not an island. In Ecclesiastes 4:9-12 we read:

> Two people are better off than one, for they can help each other succeed. If one person falls, the other can reach out and help. But someone who falls alone is in real trouble. Likewise, two people lying close together can keep each other warm. But how can one be warm alone? A person standing alone can be attacked and defeated, but two can stand back-to-back and conquer. Three are even better, for a triple-braided cord is not easily broken.[68]

These and many other suggestions I have studied over the years have infused a value of community—sticking together—and as a member of community, I assume responsibility for others.

It is probably safe to say that individuals pick up on the responsibility to self and others at different times or stages of life. While I think I assumed responsibility relatively early, I'm sure I didn't give it much thought because its emergence was somewhat subtle and had a gradual, cumulative effect. While there may well have been an experience earlier that got my attention, there is no question that the following scenario describes a defining moment that I will remember forever.

---

68. Ecclesiastes 4:9-12, NLT.

It was a Wednesday evening in October 1958. I had just begun my junior year as a pharmacy student, celebrated my twentieth birthday and was working that evening at Oakman's Drug Store in Charleston. The store included a pharmacy, the usual "front merchandise," and a soda fountain. Doc (J. E.) Whittle was the store owner and thoroughly enjoyed "Wednesday Night Poker" at the country club. There was no one available to "cover" the pharmacy that evening, and he turned to me: "Can you handle the pharmacy if I go to the game?" I was not forthcoming with a positive answer, which gave him enough time to continue: "I've watched you fairly closely since you've been working here. You seem to be pretty levelheaded, handle our customers very well, and must be a decent student or you wouldn't be in your third year." I was yet to make a comment when he said: "I will stay until 6 o'clock and leave the store with you to oversee the other employee, cover the pharmacy, and close at 9 o'clock. You'll be OK... There shouldn't be many, if any prescriptions to come in after I leave because most of the physicians' offices are closed for the day." He gave me his contact information and left for the poker game.

Just before closing, a patient, clearly uncomfortable, came in with her prescription. I read the prescription carefully, numerous times, and knew exactly what it called for. I was also fairly certain that she would be much more comfortable if she had the medication prescribed that night rather than the next day. I made the irresponsible decision to fill the prescription, allowing her to go home to a good night's sleep. Honestly, I felt pretty proud, even smug!

After closing the store, I went home (to the dormitory), "hit the books" for a couple of hours and went to bed. Around 3:00 a.m. I was awakened and was covered with a cool sweat. I don't know what caused me to rouse but I immediately began second-guessing my decision to fill that prescription. After dressing at that early hour, returning to the pharmacy and reliving the event, from the moment the patient gave me the prescription until she left with her medication, I was reassured—she got the correct medication along with proper directions.

Two thoughts came to mind as I drove back to the dorm: The patient's condition was not life-threatening, and had I made a mistake in selecting the correct medication, it could have been a new challenge she did not deserve. The law did not permit me the privilege of filling a prescription at this stage of training without direct supervision of a pharmacist—the consequences could have been to never practice the profession. This experience impressed upon me the extreme value of making wise and responsible decisions, knowing that someone's life may be in the balance.

As I think about what I have written above, I am reminded how casually we approach life's responsibilities. Thus, I advise to fear the casual mindset that answers life with lines such as "No big deal," "Someone else will take care of it," and "It's just an accident," as it often betrays a frivolity that belies the sanctity of life and denies the great power of choice that lies within us. Hours after I had filled that prescription, my conscience brought to my attention that my pride had superseded the degree of respect I should have had for this lady's life, as well as the system in place for my training as a pharmacist. The humble leader must conquer their human desires for self-aggrandizement with a greater sense of respect and responsibility for others. The Navy Ceremonial Guard had been given responsibility for honoring the individual who had given his life for his country, and thus, he performed his duties in accordance with the monumental respect he had for the servicemen at Arlington Cemetery. Reed Peterson had more than earned my respect for the news he had come to tell me and the grief he was bearing, but because I chose to cater to the interest of my team and was consumed with the fear of losing the project, I blinded myself to the visible signs that something was clearly wrong with Reed. Ed Lawhorn taught me from an early age how a great man recognizes raw talent and respects the value that every individual brings to the table—from asking my fifteen-year-old opinion on what colors to paint his store, to encouraging me to pursue education as a pharmacist, to paying close attention to the challenges I faced and seeking to support my endeavors (as he did with the gift of a car rather than allowing me to buy a motorbike, which he deemed unsafe). Michael Yost's speech was delivered to call us to reflect on how we got to where we are; his respect for the impact of the giants in his life encouraged the audience to become giants in the lives of others.

The power and beauty in these stories would be crushed if an ideology of "I am my own island" was given room to grow or self-aggrandizement took priority in these men's lives. We will be humbled by the fruit that comes from boldly taking responsibility and becoming thoroughly enmeshed in the lives of others. Could we aim to develop our own talents, not for our own egos, but so that we can be the shoulders others stand upon?

APPLICATION QUESTIONS:

- Do you accept the responsibility that accompanies your sovereignty, self- determination and freedom to choose? If yes, explain your understanding of personal responsibility and give two or three examples that demonstrate your understanding.

- Share your understanding of self-respect and respect for others.

- We do things for our own reasons. What does this statement mean to you, and how does it relate to humble leadership?

- Considering the statement "standing on the shoulders of giants," on whose shoulders do you now stand and who could stand upon your own shoulders? What future impact do you think you could have on those whose stand on your shoulders, and how could you launch them to future successes?

CHAPTER 7: Values Aligned with Actions: *Authenticity Builds Trust*

While many think that "vision" is of high importance, and I think it is, it pales in comparison to instilling trust. I have previously referenced the study done by Tom Rath, Barry Conchie, and The Gallup Organization,[69] having to do with why we follow others. They interviewed around 10,000 people and found that trust is one of the four primary reasons why they follow someone else; the most influential leaders instill a sense of trust in their followers.

A number of years ago I was facilitating a workshop that included a discussion of values. I asked the question, "Is truthfulness a non-negotiable value?" One answer was, "All values are negotiable, including truthfulness." After getting over the shock, I began accepting the notion that we are living in a post-modern, relativistic age, and many people no longer esteem absolute truth. In fact, I just learned that Oxford Dictionaries announced "post-truth" as their 2016 word of the year. I understand that to tell the "truth and nothing but the truth" is difficult; there is a tendency to make the truth what one wants it to be, and some will claim it is impossible to complete a 24-hour period and be completely honest. Make no mistake, however, truth continues to be the best policy!

Truth has become what a person wants it to be (i.e. subjective), and this permits one to steer clear of tradition and any external authority. People say

---

69. Rath, Tom, and Barry Conchie. Strengths Based Leadership: Great Leaders, Teams, and Why People Follow. Gallup Press, 2009.

they get to define for themselves what's true, good, and beautiful, but it's all relativistic—true for you but not for me, they will say. However, this philosophy validates a natural desire to cling to our confirmation biases and can blind us to facts in the world around us and truth offered by others. Mr. Vitale says we are afraid of truth. In his view, "Truth has so often been abused that experience has taught us the trajectory of truth—the trajectory of believing you are right, and others are wrong—is from truth to disagreement to devaluing to intolerance to extremism to violence to terrorism."[70] Do you agree?

In the following pages, I will discuss the intrinsic relationship between trust and trustworthiness, how one establishes trustworthiness in the eyes of others, and how one rebuilds trust once it is lost.

It is my wholehearted belief that we cannot divorce a discussion of trustworthiness from truth; to be true, to be trustworthy is one and the same. Trustworthiness is that trait that encourages anyone to have confidence, faith, or hope in us. The key to trusting a person is knowing that person, because without the vulnerability of openness and a willingness to drop your walls and let others in, an authentic self cannot be known and counted on. Of course, we can only begin to be open about our strengths, weaknesses, and goals when we recognize and acknowledge them in ourselves first. This is one of the main reasons I suggest to others that they complete the "Big Five" assessment and a 360 evaluation, both of which I describe in more detail in the appendix. These assessments permit one to know herself or himself and provide a framework for sharing that knowledge with others.

Trust in another begins as a stimulus to one's senses. Thus, many of us physically prepare and are conscious of how we present ourselves: how we dress, how we stand, our gestures and mannerisms, etc. Humble leaders must keep these important factors in mind when seeking to be seen as trustworthy and when promoting this trait in those they lead. Individuals who are readily recognized as trustworthy thoughtfully consider the value of sociocultural norms and show them the due respect, whether they be

---

70. ibid.

deemed sacred or are simply expected. In this way, one's physical presentation acts as a reflection of their trustworthy spirit, character, and attitude. When do we deem someone as trustworthy? The perception we have of one's trustworthiness matures when continuous observations and personal interactions establish that initial perceptions are real and can be used to anticipate the other person's behavior. Our assessment of someone's trustworthiness can be affected by our own biases and limited perception of them, and to offset this, we must allow enough pliability and margin of error in our estimation of others. Otherwise, we will undoubtedly set ourselves up for disappointment, when others do not meet our standards, in order to allow for growth in others and our relationships.

Can we assume trustworthiness is an innate quality of an individual? If our default behavior is "me first," does that imply that we ourselves are trustworthy or trust others? Of course not! If we want to be known as being trustworthy, we have to choose early and often the behaviors that give rise to such character. Mr. Vitale's thoughts on trust above imply that many see or accept trust on a "scale," even if we do so unintentionally—a few little white lies are acceptable as long as they are not overdone. We must give the impact of these little white lies a great deal of serious thought. Jordan Peterson has said frequently that it is very difficult, if not impossible, for any of us to complete a twenty-four-hour period without telling a lie! Can you do it?

Austin Dacey wrote an opinion that appeared in *The New York Times* on February 3, 2006. His opinion, titled, "Believing in Doubt," included the statement, "Surely many moral duties are defeasible and, in that sense, relative. We all recognize that although lying is typically wrong, under certain circumstances—to protect someone's life, for example—it is justifiable." [71] While I fully understand the view that lying is acceptable when the resulting consequences maximize benefit or minimize harm, I disagree that lying is the best option, even under such circumstances. To be sure, the "white lie" is expedient and often yields the desired results. However, it remains a lie, and there is often a better, albeit sometimes more laborious

---

71. Dacey, Austin. Opinion. New York Times. Print Edition. February 3, 2006. Page A00023.

and time-consuming, way. As we establish a trusting relationship with one another—superior, peer or subordinate—the opportunity to discuss difficult issues becomes feasible. Once the immediate and long-term effects of the truth are understood, the state of things as they actually are becomes apparent, and the acceptance of hard truths becomes a viable option. Dallas Willard shed a little light on this issue when he wrote, "Truth reveals reality, and reality can be described as what we humans run into when we are wrong!"[72] Along with others who have lived in the 20th and early 21st century, I have experienced the emergence of what we call the postmodern society, a movement characterized by broad skepticism and subjectivism, and one in which everything is relative, i.e., no absolute morality, no absolute truth, nor absolute goodness. Having been aware of and enmeshed in this movement of doubts and reservation, I have reached the conclusion from my own experiences that if we live a "relativistic life"—one of no absolutes and one that assumes reality is what we want it to be—we will eventually come face-to-face with an absolute. Specifically, once we assume truth or other virtues are relative, we eventually experience reality, which tells us we are absolutely wrong.

If we don't meet the criteria for trustworthiness, what must we do? If we happen to make a wrong choice and damage our trustworthiness with others, what can we do? These are great questions, and I have gotten them many times over the years. In the unfortunate event that we have broken someone's trust, for whatever reason, we must accept the fact and take responsibility. Commitment to being trustworthy in the face of suspicion has to become the name of the game. Trust is indeed fragile and is built in elusive ways; consistent trustworthy behavior will build the framework for trust to be rebuilt, but it may take years, decades, or a lifetime. It is human nature to always see the single crack in a sturdy wall; the key to your endurance is letting your desire to be a trustworthy person be your goal—if the specific person can learn to trust you again, that is a bonus.

72. Willard, Dallas. *The Allure of Gentleness: Defending the Faith in the Manner of Jesus.* HarperOne, and Imprint of HarperCollins Publishers, 2015.

Dr. John Blakey in his book, *The Trusted Executive,* explains how to develop and measure organizational trust, handle trust violations, and manage a constantly changing work environment and diverse workforce. The following list of nine habits was derived from interviews he conducted of CEOs on the topic of inspiring trust. They are a great starting point for development of trust within an organization: deliver, coach, be consistent, be honest, be open, be humble, evangelize, be brave, and be kind.[73] To learn more about building these habits to inspire trust, I highly recommend getting a hold of Dr. Blakey's book.

For further reading on the topic of trust, I highly recommend: The Stanford Encyclopedia of Philosophy. It offers a genuinely nice overview of this virtue, and while pointing out its value when forming relationships, it suggests a level of risk since people in whom we place our trust may not respond in like manner.

Keep in mind the trustworthy person is one with a firm adherence to a code of moral values and a thoughtful expression of that which is good. He or she is honest and incorruptible, steeped in truthfulness and integrity. If you aren't, start a new habit by making new choices and you can become that person.

Authenticity

Lance Secretan, born in Amersham, UK, educated at the London School of Economics and Political Science and the University of Southern California and Managing Director of Manpower Limited, is best known for his work in leadership theory and his thoughts on how to inspire teams. He once stated, "Authenticity is the alignment of head, mouth, heart, and feet—thinking, feeling, and doing the same thing—consistently. This builds trust, and followers love leaders they can trust."[74]

---

73. Blakey, John. *The Trusted Executive: Nine Leadership Habits that Inspire Results, Relationships and Reputation.* London, Kogan Page, 2016.

74. "Lance Secretan Quotes." BrainyQuote.com. BrainyMedia Inc, 2019. 5 December 2019. https://www.brainyquote.com/quotes/lance_secretan_414135.

Authenticity is defined as the degree to which one is true to one's own personality, spirit, or character, despite external pressures. In the words of Oswald Chambers, "We are only what we are in the dark; all the rest is reputation."[75] Authenticity is that aspect of a person that can be believed or accepted; what about them is trustworthy, reliable, genuine, real? If someone is observing my behavior day in and day out, will they see the same person today as they saw yesterday? Will they see the same person this morning as they saw last night? Will they see the same person away from home that they see at home? Am I the same person in a group that I am when alone? Am I the same in a traffic jam or when I'm "cut off" as when the traffic is moving freely? In the end, I ask: *Am I authentic?*

As I reflect on the definition of authenticity above, I think of the challenges my "authentic self" and its values encounter daily as a result of living in a material world with unexpected influences. Consider your own daily intentions and the influences that often disrupt those intentions—Are you authentic? If someone is looking for you to lead them, are they looking in the right direction? Can someone count on your being the same tomorrow and always? Do you follow through on your promises to yourself and others? We must be vigilant in maintaining our values—to maintain our true selves—in the face of countless distractions and frustrations.

Personal integrity must be discussed when considering authenticity. Personal integrity emerges where ethics, a collection of behaviors that influence how one should live, and morality, a lived standard—the way one actually lives, overlap. Therefore, I contend that the more authentic a person, the higher is their level of personal integrity. People want their leaders to be authentic—mean yes when they say yes and mean no when they say no.

"Know thyself" suggests we should avoid making a "self-assessment" that exceeds who we are and ignore the opinions of others. This aphorism also suggests that authentic behavior requires us to know ourselves and determine if the "self" we know is the "self" we want to be. Lao Tzu, a Chinese Taoist philosopher stated that mastering others is a strength; mastering

---

75. Chambers, Oswald. *The Love of God.* Fort Washington, Christian Literature Crusade, 1985.

yourself is power.[76] The "Big Five Aspects Scale"[77] mentioned earlier, is an incredibly helpful tool for understanding one's strengths and weaknesses, and provides information regarding *openness, conscientiousness, extroversion, agreeableness,* and *neuroticism.* Information collected over the years strongly suggests that self-knowledge is related to success in the workplace, as well as life in general. Self-knowledge as it relates to these five aspects is crucial for understanding how we will naturally relate to others and how we can improve relations with those that differ from us. We have further information on the "Big Five Assessment" in the appendix as well as the "360 Assessment" in full. While the Big Five Assessment is performed by yourself, the 360 will tell you how you come across to others. Armed with both of these assessments, the humble leader will be mightily equipped to pursue their goals and assist in the flourishing of others. The authentic humble leader knows who they are, evaluates the impact their behavior has on others, and decides whether that impact on others was worthwhile. In other words, when we leave the presence of someone else, do we and the other person or persons feel better about ourselves because of the encounter?

As I close this chapter, make note that I have discussed trust and authenticity together because in my opinion, they are inextricably linked, i.e., the trustworthy person is inclined to be authentic and, conversely, the authentic person is inclined to be trustworthy. These are exceedingly important traits for any individual and must not be trivialized. This being the case, I have concern when anyone suggests that these or other virtues are open in principle to revision. I suggest you exercise great care and concern when, in the interest of or respect for another person's feelings or imagined well-being, you decide to revise what you know to be true and authentic.

---

76. "Lao Tzu Quotes." BrainyQuote.com. BrainyMedia Inc, 2019. 5 December 2019. https://www.brainyquote.com/quotes/lao_tzu_130742.

77. Peterson, Jordan. Personality Assessment for Individuals. https://www.understandmyself.com/.

APPLICATION QUESTIONS

- Assignment for next session, "Select a 24-hour period and make every effort to be completely truthful—tell no lies, including white lies—for the entire period." Did you make it through without any lies?

- Once one's trust has been breached, how can the damage be repaired?

- Do you think integrity is critical to authenticity and why?

- Are trustworthiness and authenticity non-negotiable values for you and if so, why?

- What is your understanding of the relationship between authenticity and courage?

CHAPTER 8: Open, Honest, Bold: *Courage*

Courage empowers us to risk being physically or emotionally debased as we continue a given albeit worthy pursuit despite difficulties, opposition or discouragement. It tells us that we have the strength of mind that energizes us to resist the impact of outside forces that say, "It can't be done, we tried that before and it didn't work, or why bother, no one cares anyway!" This holds true whether our courage relates to intellectual, physical, moral, emotional, or other undertakings.

Courage is important because the lives of all people are difficult. Many people are very self-centered and must have things their way, which makes establishing positive relationships a challenge. Some people are hypocrites, or not always easy to get along with, or seem to take the opposite side no matter what, and we tend to shun their company! Many people are very emotional and make it nearly impossible to establish a level playing field where courteous or polite conversations can take place. Then there are those who take free will, their freedom to choose, to an incredulous level, defend it to the bitter end and refuse to listen to another point of view. As you know, this list of everyday thorns in our sides can be extended almost indefinitely. However, the humble leader recognizes the potential in these individuals and courageously chooses to go the extra mile to seek to understand, discuss, and convince them to become positive, productive and flourishing members of their communities and institutions. Courage means knowing that life is difficult, but not impossible!

The question is, "How does the humble leader become steeped in the mental prowess necessary to lead him or herself so that they may help others meet life's challenges and flourish?"

There is a useful book written by Christopher Peterson and Martin Seligman titled *Character Strengths and Virtues (CSV)*. This book classifies twenty-eight specific strengths under six broad virtues that consistently emerge across history and culture: wisdom, courage, humanity, justice, temperance, and transcendence. Following their reasoning, courage consists of five strengths:

- Bravery, which is acting rightly in the face of popular opposition, shame, scandal, discouragement, or personal loss.

- Persistence, which is maintaining perseverance despite fatigue or frustration.

- Integrity, which is the qualifications of being honest and having strong moral principles—in other words, moral uprightness.

- Vitality, which is a love and respect of life, a perspective which exhibits health and youth.

- Zest, which is living life with a sense of excitement, anticipation, and energy.[78]

Brené Brown, in her book *Braving the Wilderness* discusses courage and vulnerability. Based on her comments, all of which you will find useful as you continue your development, one may safely assume that exercising this trait is not without risk. To stand firm on a given pursuit requires an internal commitment to its value and a willingness to undergo shame, embarrassment, or a feeling of awkwardness. One antidote to the chaotic experiences that are likely to follow as you attempt to advance or defend this pursuit is to become steeped in the knowledge and understanding of its many dimensions. For example, there is always more than one side to

---

78. Christopher and Seligman, Martin. *Character Strengths and Virtues.* American Psychological Association and Oxford Press, 2004.

every story (issue), and we often approach that issue with a confirmation bias, i.e., we pick up on the parts that agree with our pre-established views and attempt to defend these views to the opposition. We end up making uninformed comments that make us feel weak, which adds to the embarrassment. To avoid this likely, show-stopping possibility, develop an open attitude and take in the whole story. While your position may not change, you are more inclined to respect the opposition's position and better able to advance your position!

Courage comes in all shapes and sizes. For some it is an innate quality and exists in sufficient supply. For others, well, you simply must learn. I believe Ms. Brown would champion us to "embrace vulnerability," whether it be economic, social, physical, or environmental. Many of us are afraid to say or do certain things. We fear moral attack, criticism, certain temptations, the onset of pain, and the list goes on. The courageous leader is well-informed, sees and understands the "big picture," and acts correctly in the right place at the right time. He accepts the risk of possible shame or embarrassment in the face of popular opposition and knows that bad things often turn out to be good and a better outcome will always come to pass.

Many years ago, I read one of the late Charles Schulz's *Peanuts* comic strips that included a brief appearance of Lucy, one of the *Peanut* characters. As I recall, she was seated in the back row of her classroom. The teacher had written an arithmetic formula on the chalkboard and asked Lucy to come to the front of the class and explain the formula. Lucy's immediate response was to pretend she didn't hear the request.

Again, the teacher said, "Lucy, please come down and explain the formula to the rest of the class."

Lucy, reluctantly, said, "Me?"

"Yes, Lucy, you."

Lucy said, "You want me to come to the front of the room and explain that formula to the entire class?"

"Yes, Lucy, come to the front of the room and explain the formula I have just written on the chalkboard."

Lucy, slowly and with grave concern written all over her face, gets out of her chair walks to the front of the class, turns to face the "audience," and says to herself, "For the first time in my life, I believe in school prayer!"

This is vulnerability, and we learn it at a very young age!

For a number of years, I used this *Peanuts* cartoon as a metaphor to introduce vulnerability and to illustrate that it should not be feared but embraced because by doing so, it becomes innocuous.

Fear, whether real or imagined, can be a very real deterrent to pursuing our goals, and over the years, I have learned that many fears are imagined and not real. I have frequently meditated on FDR's quote: "The only thing we have to fear is fear itself," and my first real example of overcoming tangible fear was my first cross-country solo flight. I determined early in my time as a district manager for The Upjohn Company that there was a need to learn to fly small airplanes. Why? The "district" assigned to me was rural and quite large geographically, stretching from the east coast of Florida to the western border of Alabama and from north of Dublin, Georgia to the south of Gainesville, Florida. Driving was not difficult but very time-consuming. Well, I did learn to fly.

After completing flying lessons and the required "airtime," I was permitted to fly alone. A situation arose at work where I would need to commute from Jacksonville, Florida to Dublin, Georgia, and with no commercial air service available, I would need to either drive up on Sunday or fly up in the Cessna 150 trainer on Monday and return by the end of the day. You guessed it—I decided to fly.

From 2 p.m. to midnight, I was planning my flight's checkpoints and calling Jacksonville Weather and the flight control center every hour to check on an inclement weather system that was making its way toward Jacksonville. The next morning it was reported that the weather system was still stalled, and thus, the decision was made that as a student pilot, I could depart the airport at first light.

After completing the pre-flight check and just before boarding the Cessna, my flight instructor walked up and asked if I had a dime. Thinking he needed the coin for some reason, I took one out of my pocket and handed it over. He said, "Keep it… I just wanted to be sure you had one because you never know when you will be forced to land at a small airport where there is no one and nothing but a pay phone." How prophetic he was!

My "take off" from the private airport was uneventful except that I was soon in the clouds and was required to do a series of 360s. The 360s were necessary because the U. S. Naval Air Station in Jacksonville was to my south, Jacksonville International Airport was to my north and I needed to reach an altitude of 3,000 feet before crossing air traffic at Jacksonville International. I had not mentally or emotionally prepared myself to perform this maneuver, and anxiety threatened to grip me; nevertheless, I quieted the fear and remembered the 360 experience I had from recovering from stall training. From the ground, the plane looked like the head of a giant corkscrew reaching into the sky! After reaching the required altitude, I took a heading that placed me on the first leg of the flight. Even though I was flying "VFR" (Visual Flight Rules), I didn't see the ground after I reached 3,000 feet and could not see Jax International or anything else on the ground. After missing my first checkpoint, my confidence was shaken slightly and I hoped I had planned my flight plan accurately. When I missed my second checkpoint, the fear occurred to me that I could've veered into the territory known as the Okefenokee Swamp where there would be no visual checkpoints from the air for miles. Nevertheless, I trusted the time and attention to detail I had spent preparing my flight plan and remembered what my instructor had constantly reminded me during training, "Airplanes are made to fly, and they will if we don't screw them up!" Thankfully, I did not miss my third checkpoint, and I saw the ground when and where I was supposed to in Folkston, Georgia! The weather cleared as I continued toward Dublin, and I landed at the time scheduled.

After completing my business in Dublin and my pre-flight check for my return home, I went over to the FBO (Fixed Base Operation) to take another look at Jax weather. It didn't look good. While still stalled, the weather system could move towards Jax at any moment. Believing I might be able to capitalize on this time while it was still stalled, I decided to "give it a shot!" Remember, this is still Monday, and I needed to return to Jacksonville because of an early flight Tuesday morning to attend a meeting in Miami. While in Dublin's FBO, I contacted Macon Control for a final weather check. As soon as the person to whom I was speaking learned I was a student pilot, without letting me finish my sentence, he said: "STAY PUT… WE BURY STUDENT PILOTS WHO IGNORE OBVIOUS HAZARDOUS WEATHER!" After he calmed down and began listening again, I presented the argument that the weather was just fine between Dublin and fifty or so miles north of Jacksonville, and I proposed to fly radio-to-radio, land at Alma, Georgia, for a final weather check and discuss with personnel in the "Radio Shack" whether to continue the flight. I further planned to rely on the radio transmitters at small airports along the way, which would equip me to land within 15 minutes almost anywhere, and the Cessna was equipped with an instrument that indicated when the plane was heading [to] and departing [from] a radio signal, which would reroute me if I could no longer rely on my pre-prepared flight plan. Considering the reasonableness of my plan and the fact that the weather front was still stalled, my "colleagues" at Alma and I decided I could continue to Waycross, Georgia—one step closer to Jacksonville and a car ride to the city if necessary. The officials at Alma were now excited by my endeavor, commenting that they wish they had the guts to do it!

As I approached Waycross, my altitude was about 2,500 feet, I could see the town, and the weather seemed to be holding. I was watching the "directional instrument" and waiting to learn exactly where I was located when I saw the Waycross Airport. By now I was close enough to Jacksonville International to initiate communication with Jax Radio. After advising them of my current location, I decided to continue the flight to the little airport at Folkston, Georgia, and advised Jax Radio accordingly. Jax Radio acknowledged my transmission and relayed traffic and weather information.

Soon after the above communication, a heavy mist began falling on the windshield, and in short order, the mist turned to rain. By the time I had descended to 1,500 feet, I was too low to communicate with Jacksonville Radio, and I was left all alone. Surprisingly I was not afraid, I was confident and in control of my plane, and it never crossed my mind that I may not make a safe landing in Folkston. I continued to descend to 1,000 feet, where I was now close enough to the ground to read road signs on the interstate. I followed I75 until the road-sign identified the exit to the airport and made a 25 degree turn to the west.

Having landed at the Folkston Airport one time during my training, I had some idea as to what to expect. There was a single, relatively short runway, with tall Georgia Pines at each end, which would require one to apply full flaps on final approach and essentially "dive" to the ground—making for a more nerve-racking and challenging landing. My landing was a good one—they all are if you walk away—and I taxied to what I remembered was the hanger. It was dark, raining, no one was around, and all I could find was a pay telephone; the dime my flight instructor had told me to keep allowed me to call him in Jacksonville to update him and arrange my return. My story did not end here however; as it turned out, I would not be driving back to Jacksonville, but flying with my flight instructor who was flown there by another instructor. He insisted that I fly the plane back myself and book this experience as an IFR (instrument flight rule) lesson. I felt confident following the directions of the tower, which included a combination of different headings and altitudes, so that Jax Radio could monitor my progress on the radar. In an effort to keep my confidence up as a student pilot, while flying in the dark and in the rain, the person in the control tower asked me to take a look to my right as he turned on the lights of a runway, which was located about halfway between Folkston and Jacksonville. I saw these lights and continued to follow his instructions, the next sight that was clear to me was when the wheels of my plane splashed the water on the runway. I had said before that even when I missed the two checkpoints earlier in the day and lost communication with the tower before being able to land in Folkston, I had complete confidence in my abilities and my instruments and felt no fear. However, when I saw those lights appear out of the stormy darkness and saw the splash of the water when my wheels touched the ground, it suddenly became crystal clear to me that it was more than my abilities, my levelheadedness that had gotten me safely home; I felt certain that someone else was in that plane besides myself and my instructor. Without that moment, I might have advised that all it took to be courageous was to plan and prepare well, keep a level head, and trust in one's abilities. Now I believe courage finds greater roots when it taps into a wellspring of confidence, greater than could be provided by one's own convincing. I made it home safely, but it was the significance of this divine intervention where I realized my confidence in myself was not enough to have achieved this feat that still strikes the core of me as I recount this memory.

People want to put their trust in a courageous leader—a person who if he says he can do something, delivers—and my first personal experience of this was my very first time sailing. Billie, our two children, and I had taken our small power boat to Grand Haven, Michigan. As we were leaving for our home port (South Haven, MI) we saw a sailboat coming through the waterway, entering Lake Michigan. She was a beautiful sight to be seen— lots of heavy, highly polished brass, brightwork of teak, constructed in the Old World style, sails full of wind—a vessel that would easily circle the globe! Our desire to be proud owners of such a watercraft peaked immediately. However, having no sailing experience and a tight budget, we quickly dismissed the idea.

As you boat owners may expect, the memory lingered, and the next summer we took step one and rented a sailboat from a source in Holland, Michigan. The source did not know that we had no experience, didn't ask, and I didn't say. Two other very courageous couples with no experience— one was my boss and his wife, the other another person who outranked me in the company and his wife—agreed to share in facing our fears and joined in the venture. Although they outranked me in the company and knew I had no sailing experience, they had confidence in me and respected that I was an accurate judge of my own abilities—I believed we could do this, and that was enough for them. Furthermore, I always sought to be as well-prepared as possible, and I was well known for this trait. Since storms moved quickly across Lake Michigan and could appear out of nowhere and meet a boat before one could turn and make for port, it was not uncommon for several boats to become swamped by a following sea every season. In order to avoid such an outcome, I had intentionally made multiple excursions during stormy weather in a small power boat. These experiences helped me get a feel for how the boat would respond in such conditions and allowed me to practice maneuvering the boat to keep the waves from overtaking.

As it turned out, our excursion was less eventful than the scenarios I had prepared for, and we were able to leave the dock without incident. We entered Lake Michigan and due to very calm seas with light wind, found ourselves two hours later back at the dock. Since this was a first-time sailing experience for all, we taught ourselves the mechanics by pulling, pushing, turning and twisting every trinket on that boat. We thoroughly enjoyed the experience, now considered ourselves "old salts," and returned home with great memories and absolutely no fear of sailing. While we had been lucky enough to experience calm seas, we were all thankful I had the experience necessary to handle the boat in stormy weather should it arise and could thus enjoy our day on the water, resting in that comfort. A huge part of courage is finding creative ways to assuage risks and committing time and resources to prepare for eventualities, even if you cannot simulate the exact details of the situation. It was this trait that our companions relied on and made them willing to undertake this adventure with us.

———————

Courageous experiences can be cumulative; one fear conquered prepares you with the wherewithal and practical wisdom to conquer the next. Therefore, it is critical to commit these experiences to memory, to make the details of how you handled a crisis indelible, so that you can draw upon them when need arises. During this final story on a sailing excursion on a vessel we owned and very similar to the one we saw in Grand Haven, Michigan, I had to draw on both of these prior stories to keep a level head and bring us back safely to shore.

This is a "harrowing" story about a trip my wife, Billie, another couple, and I took across Lake Michigan. Before I go any further, let me say that one of the most courageous people I know is Billie. She has taken many chances with me over the years and was always my source of encouragement! The following is just one of those chances.

The sailboat, carrying the name *Quintessence*, was manufactured by Hans Christian. The shipyard was on the Island of Taiwan, which is roughly 100 miles off the coast of southeastern China. *Quintessence* was a center-cockpit cutter with a 48-foot hull and an overall length of approximately 60 feet. Her home port at the time was South Haven, Michigan, which is located on the Southeastern Coast of Lake Michigan.

It was midsummer, and my brother Tom and his wife, Janelle, from Greenville, South Carolina, had joined Billie and me for a cruise from our port in South Haven, Michigan to Milwaukee, Wisconsin, Chicago, Illinois, then back to South Haven. We had an early dinner in town, then bedded down for a couple of hours before departing around midnight. Gathering on deck at the appointed time, we made ready for departure and exited the channel to Lake Michigan shortly thereafter. We set our course for Milwaukee, which is around 100 miles west and a little north of South Haven. Underway for less than an hour, beneath what appeared to be a clear sky, a slight mist began falling and the wind became calm. Not knowing what exactly to expect from the weather, we dropped the sails (there were three—jib, stay, and main), donned our foul weather gear and decided to maintain our course under engine power for another hour or so before deciding to continue or return to port.

The first hour passed, as did the next and the next and the next until dawn was beginning to break. By then we were at the point of no return, more than one-half the distance of the trip. The mist had given way to a light rain, winds had increased from relatively calm to approximately ten knots from the northeast, and the calm seas had given way to a heavy chop with waves from one to three feet. Given our current location and available options, we decided to continue our planned course.

As time continued to pass, the experience during the following few hours was essentially uneventful. While not quite as comfortable as earlier as the light rain continued, the winds increased from calm to around 5 knots and the seas were beginning to build. However, it wasn't long until the seas had reached what you may define as moderate to heavy, so we put up the stay sail in hopes of gaining a little more stability. Even though the weather conditions were becoming more threatening, I was not necessarily concerned because the boat was a heavy, well-built, "seagoing" vessel. As time passed and we continued our journey, I translated the admonition from my flight instructor to, this *boat is made to sail so don't screw it up!* I knew how to handle the boat, and my "crew" was competent and engaged. My courage was bolstered by prayer and adequate training, and it gave me confidence that we would eventually arrive at the Milwaukee Harbor safely.

What a difference an hour makes! It was now around 1400, the nor'easter caused the seas to build significantly, and our eyes began playing tricks, that is, as we looked west over the horizon, there appeared to be bright sunshine and no rain. Oops! Wrong. As I stood in the boomkin, a small "platform," the furthest point aft on the boat, holding on to the backstay and looking behind me, it appeared that the peak of the swell was eight to ten feet above my head. Looking forward, sixty feet from where I was standing, the bowsprit appeared to be at least fifteen feet from the nadir of the swell. With a few quick calculations, I realized the swell was 80 feet from peak to nadir. At this time, Janelle began experiencing a little seasickness, Billie was too busy to get sick, and Tom and I were doing OK.

At around 1600, when we had been underway for just under 16 hours, the Milwaukee skyline began to appear. Assessing the influence of the current winds and sea, we estimated another two hours before making port. The seas remained the same, with tremendous swells building from the northeast as described above, but the winds had increased to a steady 15 knots, gusting to 35. We knew from the sea charts that the harbor had a north and south entrance. Considering the intensity of the seas and the northeast winds, we decided to try for the north entrance so that if we missed, we had the south entrance as a backup.

I scrambled forward, took the stay sail down and Tom began a turn from
our current westerly heading to the north. Our plan was to get the boat far
enough north of the north entrance so that when we completed the turn,
we would be on a southeasterly track and could use the direction of the sea
to help take us through the entrance. It was a good decision and eventually
worked, but not immediately. The engine stopped!

Quintessence carried two fuel tanks and was equipped with a small Yanmar
diesel engine. I knew that fuel in tank 1 was running low and tank 2 was
full. I decided not to make the switch at that time because previous experience reminded me that diesels can be finicky and switching tanks during
turbulent times may allow air to enter the fuel lines. Diesels will not run
when there is air in the lines. So now what?

The engine was quiet, we were quiet, and the only sounds were a northeast
wind and turbulent seas. Having the choice of hoisting the main, which
would require trimming to avoid additional danger due to heavy winds,
or trying to crank the engine, I chose the latter. Tom was still at the helm
and placed the throttle in full-open position. I went below, switched the
tanks, signaled him to try to start the engine, and prayed a very serious
prayer. Voila! The engine began running immediately. We continued the
turn, and when far enough north, we assumed a southwest heading. Our
plan worked. The heavy, following sea took us directly through the middle
of the opening and into Milwaukee's harbor. The winds were now gusting
to 45 knots and the seas were well over the top of the seawall. The seas
inside were calm!

After entering the harbor, we made a turn to the starboard (north) with the
idea of reaching the Milwaukee Yacht Club, where we were expected to be
overnight. As we continued, we saw and heard a crowd, which included
a small, assertive young lady—a college student, around 20 years of age
working a summer job at the park adjacent to the marina—standing on
the end of a pier about 50 yards forward of us. She screamed, "Bring your
boat alongside this pier and throw me a dock line!"

I responded with, "I am headed to the Yacht Club, which is further inside the basin."

She returned my comments with a most courageous scream, "You'll never make it, Captain, get in here and throw me a line that is firmly secured to your vessel."

I admit, she spoke with such courage and confident gusto, I said nothing more and advanced to where I was told! Tom threw her a line, and she secured the bow. With the winds and a small engine, it was impossible to maneuver the stern up to the pier, so we got another line over to her, placed the line around one of the boat's main winches, and winched the stern over until it was secured to the pier.

The story was not yet over however. I had gone below to help straighten up things that had moved around during the trip when someone topside yelled that the Milwaukee Harbor Police would like to speak to the captain. You can imagine what went through my mind after this long, unbelievable day!

I went topside and onto the pier where I was face-to-face with what appeared to be six or seven "giants" in police uniforms. The spokesman for the group said, "Captain, we got a call from an unknown individual up the beach who said there was a boat offshore that seemed to be in serious trouble… that he could see the vessel and hear radio transmissions when on the peak of the swell but could not see nor hear anything when it went down. We immediately came to the marina, made our boats ready but were afraid to come out. We apologize and are happy you are safely in port. Welcome to Milwaukee."

I reflected on the foregoing for years and the courage required by these events is unmatched in my lifetime. I was prepared for this moment by the myriad of similar, if less challenging experiences of my life, where I had paid attention to what was needed and acted accordingly. Tommy Lasorda, retired manager of the LA Dodgers, once stated: "There are three types of baseball players: those who make it happen, those who watch it happen, and those who wonder what happens." Like baseball players and sailors, humble leaders must be in the game and make it happen. My closing message is that as life threatens to pass you by, pay attention to it, recognize what its challenges demand of you, and act accordingly with courage.

It was Edmund Burke, statesman, author, orator, political theorist, philosopher and member of parliament, who gave us the statement: "The only thing necessary for the triumph of evil is for good men to do nothing."[79] Triumphing over evil takes courage. E. E. Cummings once wrote, "It takes courage to grow up and become who you really are."[80] Earlier in this book I wrote that authenticity is the degree to which one is true to one's own personality, spirit, or character, despite external pressures—that is, you are the same, day or night, in public or behind closed doors. To do so, my friend, is no easy task. When the door to vulnerability opens, risk floods in and mechanisms of fear automatically engage.

In the opinion section of the *New York Times*, a David Brooks article was published, "The Courage of Small Things." In this article, he describes the beginning of a shrinking world for Clemantine Wamariya, age 6, who witnessed the beginning of genocide in Rwanda. He described inconceivable situations: her father had to stop going to work after dark for fear of rampant murderers wandering the countryside; her family ate dinner in the dark so no passersby knew they were home; the family had to move from house to house to maintain mobility and avoid being recognized; she and her sister were once told to flee and upon seeing dead bodies floating down the river thought they were simply people sleeping. All of which she and her sister, Claire, had to deal with as they escaped. At the end of the article, he stated:

> Based on his account of the story, Clementine, as a young girl, was exceptionally courageous and had the strength to face the horrific, absolute brutality of genocide. Even though the memory of these experiences were inked in her memory, never to be forgot-

79. "Edmund Burke Quotes." BrainyQuote.com. BrainyMedia Inc, 2019. 5 December 2019. https://www.brainyquote.com/quotes/edmund_burke_377528.

80. "e. e. cummings Quotes." BrainyQuote.com. BrainyMedia Inc, 2019. 5 December 2019. https://www.brainyquote.com/quotes/e_e_cummings_161593.

ten, she had developed a level of maturity to carry on, escape this cruelty, and move forward with the assurance that there is a better tomorrow.

This young girl acted with incredible bravery through challenges most of us will hardly be able to cognize, let alone will ever have to endure. Remember, courage is the first of human qualities because it is the quality that guarantees all the others. It is truly worth building into your character, and I strongly suggest you take a look at your fears, understand them as best you can, and develop a way to eliminate them. Your fears are still worthy of being conquered, even if they do not involve great personal tragedy or epic adventures. For example, many people have a fear of speaking before a large audience. One approach to overcoming this fear is to prepare a brief speech—a story about yourself is easy and a good start—and present the "speech" to three or four willing subjects. After repeating this process a few times, add information to your content, maybe increase the number of subjects and before you know it, your level of comfort will have increased enough to "go public." Once you face your first big audience, remember that you know your subject and are speaking to one person in the audience at a time.

To be sure, courage is important and can be learned. Break the "fear project" down into small parts, face it, learn about it, conquer it, and go forward!

APPLICATION QUESTIONS:

• Explain the relationship between courage and risk.

• How would you explain the importance of courage in your institution to your followers and instruct them as to how it may be developed?

• What is your understanding of the relationship between courage and narcissism—are they complementary or antithetical?

• Share your understanding of Brené Brown's statement, "The foundation of courage is vulnerability."

PART III
The Humble Leader in Action

CHAPTER 9: Priorities in the Culture You Create: *First Things First*

In this chapter, we will discuss the critical aspects of a flourishing community that a leader must prioritize in the culture he or she creates: diversity, inclusion, and tolerance; adaptability and flexibility; creativity and innovation; patriotism and citizenship; self-discipline, temperance, and stability; critical thinking, strategic thinking, and problem solving; integrity; and perseverance. The previously discussed core virtues should naturally promote and support the following values, which in turn will instill great confidence in the watching follower. These values should not require our daily attention, but rather happen at the unconscious level. How do these values become instinctual? Whether it be a skill or a value, there are four stages to learning. Stage one is referred to as unconscious incompetence. This simply means that we don't know what we don't know. Stage two is conscious incompetence. In this stage, we are aware of the fact that we are at the beginning of a long learning curve. This stage requires commitment and the personal decision to follow through. Stage three is conscious competence. You are now aware of significant improvement in a given area but know more work is to be done. The final stage is unconscious competence. When you reach this state, you can perform a skill effortlessly. This stage allows us to enter an absorbed, thoughtless state. In this stage, we do things we want to do or should do without thought or conscious effort. Our critical, cultural values should exist and be applied at a stage four level of competence. For example, we should not have to think about being polite. It should come naturally.

Diversity and Inclusion

A few weeks ago, I facilitated a workshop at the University of Maryland School of Pharmacy relevant to the pharmaceutical industry. There were approximately ten students in the class who were working towards their Ph. D. in pharmaceutical health services research. As I sat with the class, observed each individual, heard the sounds of their voices, and listened to their responses to various topics being discussed, I became richly aware that this was truly a diverse group. There were females and males in the group and not one of the students was native to the United States. It also became abundantly clear that if there was to be a successful outcome of our time together, it was necessary both that this diversity be recognized and features common among us be found in our exchange of views in order to establish common grounds for understanding. While it is easy to yield to the temptation in the presence of a younger group to pose as the all-knowing, smart guy who reduces the thoughts of a room into a single one liner, the humble leader must commit him or herself to being a resource of knowledge to be shared and built upon. This leader should derive their satisfaction from becoming more informed and should encourage others to find their voice in the discussion.

Diversity is the representation of fairness and protection to all, regardless of gender, race, religion, ethnicity, or sexual orientation. Inclusion in the business environment integrates individuals of all of the above demographics into one workplace, and supports a collaborative environment that values open participation from individuals with different ideas and perspectives that have a positive impact. Leadership at such an organization that is inclusive encourages communication and engagement.

Without question, diversity and inclusion is a leadership issue throughout all institutions today. Increasingly, employees are operating as a network of teams, and these teams support a collaborative environment where different ideas and perspectives are valued. These teams respond to empowerment, transparency, open dialogue, as well as inclusive and engaging working styles. Leading organizations see diversity and inclusion both as a mandate and the instrument by which to increase employee engagement, improve employee experience, and enhance performance. Effective leaders take full ownership of diversity and inclusion in their communities and encourage acceptance among colleagues at all levels. Leaders of every age and level of experience must be flexible and be able to bow to others' views; this does not necessarily mean that you need to change your own opinion, but simply learn from the opinion of others. He or she must be willing to seek out the potential latent in others and provide the milieu in which these individuals can become leaders in their own right.

In a nutshell, the humble leader embraces the value of diversity in all people and effectively motivates them, whatever their culture or background. In order to do this genuinely, the leader must actively broaden his or her knowledge of other perspectives through intentional interactions with people outside their daily sphere of influence by expanding their knowledge of languages through travel and study, as previously discussed in our section on wisdom. Only then will the humble leader have a true appreciation for the value of diverse views and opinions and will be able to effectively help others appreciate this value.

Tolerance

There was a time when my wife and I lived in New York City, just a few blocks northwest of the United Nations. As I walked by that building, I would note with interest the many countries represented by the people I saw. Today, as I enter the campus of our academic institutions and "multinational" businesses, the people I see remind me of the United Nations. People from all over the world are there. And, foremost in my mind is the social tool all leaders need in their toolbox is the ability to be tolerant of others. Tolerance helps members of the institutions we serve to build bridges and capitalize on differences.

Previously in this book I referred briefly to the "Big Five" personality theory assessment. Included in that theory is an attention given to openness, one of the big five personality traits. The person exhibiting a high level of openness, among other things, enjoys trying new things, appreciates others' ideas, is curious and open minded. The tolerant person demonstrates similar behavior, and will be noted for their patience, understanding, acceptance and appreciation of differences, and their desire to learn about other people.

To be sure, there is a significant opportunity for the humble leader to make a difference. It seems that one's willingness to allow, and sometimes suffer another's behavior is an inclination of the past, a behavior we see little of today. Cultures' increasing tendency to focus on self-serving behavior, often at the expense of someone else, makes the patience and selfless nature of the humble leader a vital necessity. The humble leader's vulnerability and personal risks will grow as their dependency on others to make good decisions expands. It is important to make sure that we as leaders are totally committed to pursuing the flourishing of others in a positive, productive way rather than for personal power and privilege. To that end, the humble leader must strive for fairness and practice justice, equity and equality. As a tolerant person, we must make sure we listen and remember that not everyone is the same. We must look for ways to connect with others, help others and ourselves grow, and know the difference between popular behavior and right behavior. Only then can we exhibit a high degree of cooperation with one another and recognize the uniqueness and value of everyone within our diverse society.

Here are a few thoughts that come to mind as early steps toward achieving a tolerant attitude.

1. Place value on others.

2. Assimilate sufficient information about others—who are they?

   • Where is their place of birth?

   • What was their formal and informal education like?

   • What are the characteristics of their family relations?

   • What are their significant life experiences?

3. Who are you? There may be someone out there who finds you intolerant.

- Spend a little time getting to know yourself.

- Remember that your strengths may be weaknesses in the eyes of others.

- Ask yourself if you are truly patient?

- Assess your ego and its impact on tolerance.

4. Be courageous.

   - Say no to things that make you intolerant

   - Avoid personalizing all conversations and related experiences.

   - Demonstrate tolerance, so others will follow suit.

Continuing this list could easily accommodate several pages. My major point is, however, you have only to look at the behavior of those around you to get an idea of the importance of this quality. We need to see a greater level of tolerance in our "self-centered" society and the humble leader must set the pace. Read the literature on the subject, meditate on it and affirm that all necessary gifts are within you. Develop them!

Adaptability and Flexibility

These two terms are similar but not interchangeable. The adaptable person is not flustered by long-term changes. For example, one may ask the adaptable individual to change from working the 7:30 a.m. – 3:00 p.m. shift to the 3:30-11:00 p.m. shift. On the other hand, the flexible person is able to accept short-termed change requirements, such as taking Fridays off rather than Saturdays during a busy quarter. Some people are equally adaptable and flexible, that is, they readily adapt to change whether long term or short term, are open to new ideas, take on new responsibilities, handle pressure well and adjust their plans to meet changing needs. Genuine humility will naturally contribute to a leader's adaptability and flexibility, but they must recognize that not everyone excels in both of these traits and lead others accordingly.

Creativity & Innovation

These two words are often used in combination because it takes both "efforts" to achieve the desired endpoint. To make this a priority within the institution, the humble leader takes the risks necessary to support change and encourage creativity and innovation.

The creative person keeps all of life front and center. This person is a master at observing one's surroundings and the behavior of living things. When the opportunity presents, he or she can give an issue serious thought, draw on their storehouse of knowledge, and come up with an idea that is novel, good, and useful that often paves the way for future endeavors. Sourcing from this wealth of knowledge these individuals have stored in their brains, they are able to put together seemingly unrelated information, make connections between different ideas, and come up with solutions to new problems, or create a new plan. To paraphrase Daniel Pink, lawyer and author of well-known book *Drive*, they can now give the world something it didn't know it was missing:[81] truth.

The innovator analyzes information and current value systems and with imagination and initiative finds a way to synthesize information from multiple sources in a new context that gives it greater value. If it were necessary for me to rate myself on creativity and innovation, innovation gets the higher score. I have such a very high degree of respect for the person who comes up with new ideas that I am comfortable leaving it to those who do it well and rather devote my efforts to translating an idea or invention into something that creates value.

Different from other sets of skills, it is likely that you are not both creative and innovative in every arena and rather fall into one camp or another; this is easily remedied by seeking out others who complement your abilities. Humble leaders will do well to assess themselves relative to these skills, gather similar data regarding their followers, and lead accordingly.

---

81. Pink, Daniel H. *Drive the Surprising Truth about What Motivates Us*. Riverhead Books, 2009.

Patriotism

Even though we think of "love for country" when we think of patriotism, we may also share the same love and fidelity for our institutions and communities. There are often disagreements in families, but love and respect overcome these differences. The workplace provides ample opportunity to debate who is right and who is wrong, but a true patriot finds common ground. Church is another place where many differences of opinion prevail but the patriotic, humble leader takes the "high road" and finds a place of comfort for all. Keep these other environments in mind when we consider patriotism for one's country.

Vanessa Raffaele published an article a few years ago in Odyssey, an American internet media company in which she posits that patriotism does not exist in Italy, her homeland. In her opinion, the country's people did not celebrate who they were unless it had to do with sports, and she implied that this lack of patriotism was part of the reason why the country is not functioning.

When we witness "national turmoil," whether it be in the United States or other countries, the term "patriotism" often appears. It should be understood that differences of opinion or factions are critical to the flourishing of a democracy, and it is unhelpful to label those who disagree with us as unpatriotic or evil. Ideally, we would all love our home country and be proud to serve its wishes. Even though it may have many faults, our attitude can make it a better place for us to live and make others feel loved. While negative views may prevail, the country that protects one's freedom to have opposing views is to be revered, respected, and loved by its people. The true patriot has a love for and loyalty to her homeland and all of that for which it stands. Patriotism is a devotion to a particular place and sincere cherishing of a particular way of life, where one finds a safe and comforting home.

The humble leader can be patriotic while attempting to understand the patriotism of others who hold similar views of their own homeland. He knows and understands the true meaning of variety, respects the sources that give rise to differences (culture, ethnicity, gender etc.), and maintains a focus on the interests of others in the pursuit of mutually acceptable courses of action.

Sooner or later, patriotism will make your country a great place in which to live, your family a loving group that you are pleased to be a part of, or your place of employment an engaging place to work! This trait encourages development of a positive energy and channeling that energy in such a way that there is flourishing of the human condition and the formation of a responsible, respectful, supportive, and sympathetic community. If we maintain our intent to understand and appreciate patriotic values by learning about the culture and natural history of where we live, those with whom we live, and the institution you work for, all with the same level of interest, then we will find patriotism to be a guiding force in our lives.

Citizenship

As I walk through the buildings of many of our institutions, I will often see a banner of some sort or posters that list the values important to that institution. Occasionally, citizenship will appear on that list and I ask what that means. Answers vary but generally relate citizenship to the members of the community who exhibit civil behavior, which in turn is defined as courteous and polite responsibility. When pushed a little further, the term becomes synonymous with "civility," clearly a trait to be valued. Unfortunately, when the conversation begins to focus on whether civility characterizes my interviewee's behavior, I would usually hear some variation of, "We don't necessarily behave like that here; it's just one of our values." Something must be amiss if the values spouted everywhere around us have no bearing on daily life in a community.

We must always remember that we are not an island unto ourselves; we are a part of communities, whether we enjoy it at all points in time or not. Good citizens take responsibility for who they are, how they behave, and they respect every other member. We will naturally find faults in that community; it is easy to find behavior that we find unacceptable. As a member, it is incumbent on us to moderate our own behavior and hopefully influence that community toward more worthy ends; this is sometimes best achieved without voiced criticism, but by simply portraying a better way of life. This in essence is civility and will appear in the civil individual as unconscious behavior. Dr. George R. Kesler, in Hillsdale College's publication, *Imprimis* states regarding civility that:

> To be "civil," in ordinary usage, means to be polite, respectful, decent. It is a quality implying, in particular, the restraint of anger directed toward others. In this sense, civility is not the same thing as warmth and indeed implies a certain coolness: civility helps to cool the too hot passions of citizenship. When citizens are civil to one another despite their political [or other, added] disagreements, they reveal that these disagreements are less important than their resolution to remain fellow citizens.[82]

The coolness Dr. Kesler speaks of, stemming from the respect and value we place on our fellow members of our communities, will certainly profit them more than the heated passions of rebellion that seek to divide and ultimately alienate.

A focus on civility is a matter of shaping the individual character of the leader and those who follow. In a society that seems to exclusively worship and reward individualism, civility, to use an "old salts" sea-going vessel term, stands athwart the current ethic of self-obsession. The good citizen takes possession of his or her institution's purpose and the values that undergird that purpose. The good citizen abides by its principles, is involved in achieving its vision, serves that institution and through it, serves the community.

Self-discipline

The late President Harry S. Truman is said to have stated, "In reading the lives of great men, I found that the first victory they won was over them-

---

82. Kesler, Charles R. "Civility and Citizenship in Washington's America and Ours." *Imprimis.* Hillsdale College. https://imprimis.hillsdale.edu/civility-and-citizenship-in-washingtons-america-and-ours/Dec 2000.

selves… self-discipline with all of them came first."[83] Having read many books about great leaders myself, I have found that President Truman describes a victory common to all of them—victory over themselves. Self-discipline for many of these greats was often a first necessary step to gaining other strengths and virtues. To be sure, demonstrating hard work and controlling one's emotions, words, actions, impulses, and desires is behavior that often reflects a level of discipline. Since for some the word "discipline" is a little strong, I often use "courageous commitment."

When discipline is present as a strength, and that strength is applied to excess, it often becomes a weakness. When one has been successful in applying self-discipline, it has a tendency to produce pride, which in turn can lead to a stubborn, hard-headed, "my way or the highway" tendency. Leaders who fall into this trap will stunt creativity and growth in those they lead and will often find themselves frustrated, exhausted, and burnt out.

The courageously committed humble leaders know there will always be risks when investing in a given endeavor and are aware that these risks often give rise to varying levels of vulnerability. These leaders make a thoughtful assessment of the level of risk, embrace the vulnerability without fear, and continue to move forward with cautious confidence, thus avoiding the pitfalls of the prideful. In contrast, the highly disciplined leader who tends to move forward with less caution, usually for the purpose of "sticking to his guns," often needs to turn to "plan B," which calls for damage control.

Striving to demonstrate and maintain an excellent work ethic and controlling one's emotions, words, actions, impulses, and desires is no easy task and often requires courage and commitment! It is useful to remember that the leader in pursuit of excellence in these areas will develop a level of trust and respect on the part of followers. When this exists, slight errors in judgement and mistakes of other sorts are received with understanding, and there is almost always a rally of the troops that makes these shortcomings go away and look like good decisions! With courageous commitment,

---

83. Truman, Harry S. Brainy Quote. https://www.brainyquote.com/quotes/harry_s_truman_121205.

give the best of yourself in the interest of others—every day, whatever it takes.

Temperance

Temperance was acknowledged by early Greek philosophers as one of man's four most desirable traits, the others being wisdom, courage, and justice. This trait has to do with moderation in action, thought, feeling, or voluntary self-restraint. It is often characterized as control over excess in any form. I remember hearing from childhood, "If a little does good, a lot will do better!" True? No! Any strength or pleasing thing used in excess becomes a weakness. Too much of a "good" thing almost always portends danger. How many of our friends and loved ones, hooked on booze or some other drug, thought they had everything under control? There doesn't seem to be a "silver bullet" when it comes to controlling certain excessive behaviors. Assuming we are serious about taking full responsibility for our life and the impact it may have on others, it is useful to take an inventory of our priorities occasionally, identify the area(s) where we lack self-control, set specific and measurable goals and take step one. We must remain accountable to ourselves and the goal we have set. We should share our goal(s) with others and review our progress regularly. As we accept the need to give up what we must, remember it as you would a bad haircut—it only lasts a few weeks. We gain something we will never lose—positive encouragement to the lives of others. Even though you will need to deny yourself, in a few weeks, you can replace the "denied habit" with a new one that is positive and of much more value.

Remember! Whether you are trying to change your habits from scratch or building more discipline, all you must do is make up your mind to do so. The literature is replete with ideas, guides, or suggestions to aid your development in this area. One such source is Lesley Lyle, who when a student at Buckinghamshire New University in Wycombe, England, completed a class in Applied Positive Psychology, and, in an effort to keep her class together, suggested creating a new website called, "The Positive Psychology People." Her idea spread around the world and the website was launched on March 20, 2015. Their hope was that the website would bring together people from different ages, genders, nationalities, and cultures with a common aim—to make a positive difference in the world through the application of positive psychology. Ms. Lyle posted an article on the website titled "Developing Temperance," which thoughtfully, albeit briefly, addresses forgiveness and mercy, humility and modesty, prudence, and self-control.[84] For each topic, there is a brief "to-do" list to aid you in becoming more apt at behaving properly in regard to each of these important areas.

To develop temperance, determine that you need improvement, come up with brief statements of affirmation that reflect the desired behavior in you, repeat them without ceasing, and watch the new habit emerge.

Stability

Stability is the third of the four reasons[85] why we follow someone else. In general, the stable person is not prone to change, is levelheaded and not subject to wild swings of emotion.

Allstate Insurance Company ran an ad in 2017 titled "Accident Forgiveness."[86] This ad represents a near-perfect example of stability and the behavior I encourage all to consider emulating. The teenager politely walks into his parent's bedroom, and carefully, although limitedly, announces that he had just had a fender-bender. In a most positive way, he congratulates them on having the wisdom to have purchased such a wonderful "accident forgiveness insurance policy." Dad has a relatively stern look on his face but says nothing. Mom, with a kind look on her face, politely and without hesitation says, "Four weeks without the car." The teenager makes a quick but graceful turn and says, "OK, have a good night." End of discussion—end of story!

84. Lyle, Lesley. Developing Temperance. March 27, 2015. http://www.thepositivepsychologypeople.com/developing-temperance/.

85. Rath, Tom, and Barry Conchie. *Strengths Based Leadership: Great Leaders, Teams, and Why People Follow.* New York: Gallup Press, 2008.

86. "Grounded," Allstate Insurance. https://www.youtube.com/watch?v=zBYTIklIodE Sept 29, 2017.

How many times did you as a teenager experience a similar crisis, only to come home to a dad or mom (or both) who, without query, made the unstudied assumption that the child did something stupid, and then made the problem even bigger? How many times have you observed an employee who made an honest mistake and the "boss," without a single clarifying question, jumped to an incorrect conclusion and compounded the problem!

The stable person is steadfast and does not become a part of the problem. He or she provides a solid foundation and can be counted on in times of need. This person has consistent core values that radiate security, strength, support, and peace. He or she makes every effort to be prepared for the unexpected, finish what they start, pay attention to details, and will often enjoy having a set schedule. This behavior will give one the ability to withstand difficult situations, handle adversity, and remain productive and capable throughout the trying circumstances. Emotional stability is a significant contributor to this trait.

The characteristics of a stable person are:

1. They provide a solid foundation and exhibit constancy of character or purpose. They consistently act with a high degree of integrity, and their core values are stable.

2. They ensure the security, strength, support, and peace of an institution and its members.

3. They can always be counted on in time of need.

4. They know when to say no to requests that would only intensify the problem.

5. They understand their weaknesses and ask for help.

6. They listen with the intention of finding a solution to the problem.

As one pursues development of stability in their leadership, they begin to appreciate the need for courage because risk is involved. A common handicap of unstable leadership is insecurity. If you frequently experience self-doubt and lack of confidence—and many of us have some of these feelings from time-to-time—you may find that it is much easier to avoid certain situations than get involved. However, avoidance doesn't get us to where we want to be. So, set up a few low-risk experiences that would normally trigger your specific insecurity, give them a try, and assess your level of comfort. I view this approach a little like culture-building—new experiences, once exercised successfully, give rise to beliefs, and once your beliefs are strong enough, new habits will emerge. These new habits will become a part of who you are. It is important to get feedback on your attempts to establish these new leadership habits from people you trust. Assuming the feedback is encouraging, it is also important that you persevere and keep moving towards your goal. Another idea worth considering is "self-talk." We tend to be our own worst critic so talk back to your inner critic. If necessary, make a list of affirmations and remind yourself of all the reasons why you must be more stable, including the benefit that trait will be to others. The more value you place on stability, the greater the chances of your reaching a "higher" score on this trait!

Without question, stability is an extremely important quality of the humble leader. In our individualistic, self-centered society, we frequently are witness to individuals who are not prepared to deal with life's certain difficulties. The humble leader must be the one to whom another may turn to provide the stability necessary for making one's way through their troubled seas.

Critical Thinking

There is more information coming our way today than ever before, and much of this information is in soundbites. The person in a leadership role must be able to understand this information, analyze it objectively, and make a reasoned judgment. Whether they be observations, experiences, carefully controlled scientific studies, or thoughtful opinions from reliable individuals, potentially useful information and their sources must be subjected to scrutiny. To this end, critical thinking is essential.

The humble leader as a critical thinker has an awareness of his or her own thinking process, and engages in reflective thinking, rational thinking, decision-making. This person needs to have reached a suitable level of mental, emotional, psychological, and spiritual maturity and possess a realistic, "can-do" attitude.

The critical thinking leader can encourage similar thought processes in followers by demonstration—when new information comes along do you accept it at face value based on its source or do you find it necessary to seek out other data to confirm the findings? This will cultivate a desire in your organization to follow reason and evidence wherever it may lead, as well as a natural inquisitiveness, even-handedness, and confidence in reaching reasonable conclusions. Furthermore, they will quickly adopt a systematic approach to problem-solving. Thus we see that it is possible to influence the habits of other minds—these habits lead to action and action produces results.

Strategic Thinking

Strategic thinking influences an institution's culture and defines the manner in which people think about, assess, view, and create the institution's future.

This skill is essential when establishing the vision (what will the institution look like a number of years ahead); purpose (why do we come to work each day?); goals (major steps to be taken that will advance the institution in accordance with its vision) and other elements of a strategic plan. The following are a few skills shown to be very useful when it comes to strategic thinking:

1. Competence in logical and creative thinking

2. The ability to facilitate discussions that yield a reasonable plan and a living document that will serve as a guide for operating the institution. This calls for a general understanding of "group dynamics"

and a healthy respect for the opinion of others. This keeps others involved and inspired by seeking input without undue judgement.

3. Commitment to developing and maintaining a high level of awareness and perceptivity. Adeptness in organization, identification and interpretation of sensory and intuitional information is crucial.

4. Commitment to continuous learning. Strategic thinking is enhanced when one develops an in-depth knowledge of the industry, competition, and sees the big picture that allows one to predict change.

5. Commitment to communicating well and often. Good, frequent communications often give rise to alternative courses of action. One's willingness to change course when the situation dictates is desirable.

6. Patience when there is pressure to complete a project, i.e., willing to go back to the drawing board when necessary.

7. Maintaining a balance between creating something new and innovative and assessing reality in order to produce an honest evaluation of what is achievable.

Problem-solving

It is important that the humble leader has the ability to assess a situation and determine whether there is a problem. If there is none, he or she must exercise the skills to deal with the behavior of individuals who feel otherwise. When there is a problem, certain skills will aid in determining the nature of the problem, finding its source, clarifying and analyzing necessary information, and identifying an effective solution. These skills include:

1. The ability to see the big picture and avoid "crisis management."

2. The ability to actively listen to all involved parties without exercising premature judgement.

3. An appreciation for opinions that differ from his or her own.

4. A willingness to make a decision once sufficient information is gathered and communicating said decision in a timely manner.

Integrity

For the purposes of our discussion, I will define integrity as the firm adherence to a strict moral or ethical code, often regarded as the honesty and truthfulness or accuracy of one's actions. It is a concept of consistency of one's behaviors, values, methods, expectations, and outcomes. It is when a person says what they mean and means what they say. The late President Dwight D. Eisenhower once wrote, "The supreme quality for leadership is unquestionably integrity. Without it, no real success is possible, no matter whether it is on a section gang, a football field, in an army, or in an office."[87]

The humble leader must be steeped in integrity and thereby understand what is morally good and bad. A blog I read recently, written by Steven Mintz, Ph. D., professor emeritus from Cal Poly State University in San Luis Obispo included the following statement: "Integrity is the most important trait of leadership in our society because regardless of what other beneficial characteristics exist, people will not follow someone unless they have established trust with them." The blog continued to say that, "CFOs were asked, 'Other than technical or functional expertise, which one of the following traits do you look for most when grooming future leaders at your organization? Their responses: Integrity (33%), Interpersonal/Communication Skills (28%), Initiative (15%), Ability to motivate others (12%), Business savvy (10%), and Other/don't know (2%).'"[88] To be sure, leaders with a strong moral compass will naturally attract the attention and respect of their superiors and followers.

While making preparation to write this book, I had many conversations and read a great deal of literature on integrity, and it appeared to me that

---

87. "Dwight D. Eisenhower Quotes." BrainyQuote.com. BrainyMedia Inc, 2020. 23 January 2020. https://www.brainyquote.com/quotes/dwight_d_eisenhower_109026.

88. Mintz, Steven. "Integrity: The Most Important Trait of Leadership." Workplace Ethics Advice. https://www.workplaceethicsadvice.com/2013/02/integrity-the-most-important-trait-of-leadership-.html Feb 2013 (Blog).

this quality is no longer valued as it was a few years ago. When I dwell on the self-centered, skeptical, and doubting tendencies that plague many of us, I find it easy to reach the conclusion that our society has experienced a total collapse of integrity, because it has been gripped by fear: the fear of being candid, transparent, held accountable, truthful, or responsible. Fear is not to be ignored for it is an emotion induced by a perceived threat. According to new research published in *The Atlantic,* a well-respected periodical, we have "four 'basic' emotions… happy, sad, afraid [fear]/surprised, and angry/disgusted."[89] Following a 2005 Gallup Poll, it was reported that one of the top ten fears as reported by adolescents was fear of failure. [90] The operative word here is "perceived." While one may successfully argue that perception is a reality for some of us, the threat remains just that—a perception. However, fear of failure can be a serious condition, and a person considers the possibility of failure so intense that they choose not to take the risk. Fear is not the focus of this chapter, but I must ask: Is fear of failure the reason we tend to avoid being candid, transparent, held accountable, truthful, or responsible? Is fear the reason we have a "total collapse of integrity in the United States?" Do we no longer value integrity? The person of integrity whose intentions, decisions, and actions are shaped by their moral code probably has little to fear.

Marshall Goldsmith, a well-known bestselling author, top-rated leadership trainer, and keynote speaker, published a highly informative article titled "Demonstrating Integrity: A Key Characteristic of the Future Global Leader." In this article, he lists five major characteristics as he approaches an answer to the question, "How do I demonstrate integrity?"

Based on this repost, personal experience, and the experience of others, the first step toward demonstrating integrity is to firmly establish the value you place on actions worthy of trust and make it clear to your followers that you live according to your morals—

---

89. Beck, Julie "New Research Says There Are Only Four Emotions." *The Atlantic.* Feb 2014. https://www.theatlantic.com/health/archive/2014/02/new-research-says-there-are-only-four-emotions/283560/.

90. Lyons, Linda. "What Frightens America's Youth?" Gallup News. March 2005 https://news.gallup.com/poll/15439/what-frightens-americas-youth.aspx.

truth, freedom, respect—and adhere to a set of principles that govern your behavior. Remember that you are constantly leading, that others are watching, and that your ethical standards are always on display. Keep your communications factual and truthful, and be willing to speak up, even when doing so may be risky. Avoid associating with any activity that encourages dishonest or unethical behavior.

Step two calls for performing to the highest ethical standards throughout the entire organization is expected. Lead each other in such a way that all personnel feel comfortable expressing concerns regarding "bad behavior." Keep all personnel reminded that the organization operates best when there are good relationships among all employees and that good relationships thrive on honesty, fairness, respect, and trust.

The third step personifies humble leadership in that it avoids political and self-serving behavior. This is easily demonstrated by being competent in doing what you are supposed to do, sharing challenges, opportunities, and recognition with fellow workers. Take comfort in being part of an others-oriented team, and recognize and avoid the many forms in which politics may appear. Make sure your fellow employees are aware of and understand all job requirements and methods of measuring performance.

Step four for demonstrating integrity includes having the courage to uphold that which you believe in and take risk when necessary. This is achieved by knowing "the territory," developing a positive attitude that will be necessary when facing opposition, and eliciting support of key colleagues. Keep in mind that as you move toward success, others are encouraged to speak up and voice their approval. Going forward, remember that supporting others when necessary will secure supporting relationships.

The fifth approach to demonstrating integrity is through expressing, by acts and deeds, your passion for the organization's values.

The first step is easy! Walk the talk, i.e, let your fellow workers see what you want them to be. As you make sure your performance exemplifies the highest standards, you will actually coach employees to follow you by acknowledging their unique knowledge, understanding, and talents. This encourages others to see the organization as a "best place to work."

If you commit yourself to becoming a person of integrity and do the necessary work, you will have given your institution and your followers a great gift that no one can take away.

Perseverance

Newt Gingrich wrote that "Perseverance is the hard work you do after you get tired of doing the hard work you already did."[91] That statement reminded me of a quote I saw on a plumber's truck the other day, "You must never get tired of doing the right thing!" In a sense, pursuing worthy objectives with discipline, determination, and patience while exhibiting fortitude when confronted with failure is a good definition of perseverance. The question is—how do we make that pursuit a "way of life," and a part of our habits and beliefs?

Perseverance is an important key to success. Any endeavor can present opportunities for failure. However, it is important to keep in mind Thomas Edison's comment, "I have not failed, I just found ten thousand ways that won't work."[92] There is an endless list of other great achievers that found that success inevitably arrives for everyone who perseveres. The name of one such great achiever that always comes to mind is Churchill. During a visit to Harrow School in October, 1941, he made the well-known statement, "Never, never, never, never–in nothing great or small, large or petty–never give in, except to convictions of honor and good sense. Never yield to

91. "Newt Gingrich Quotes." BrainyQuote.com. BrainyMedia Inc, 2020. 23 January 2020. https://www.brainyquote.com/quotes/newt_gingrich_107062.

92. "Thomas A. Edison Quotes." BrainyQuote.com. BrainyMedia Inc, 2020. 23 January 2020. https://www.brainyquote.com/quotes/thomas_a_edison_132683.

force. Never yield to the apparently overwhelming might of the enemy."[93] When you give your word, tough it out if humanly possible! When there comes a time when you want to quit, remember a time when perseverance paid off, it will give you the courage to continue.

Inc. published a nice little summary written in "step-by-step" fashion by Jessica Stillman[94] that will help us build the habit of perseverance. In her words, "The brave aren't fearless, they just do the right thing *despite* their fear. The same goes for resilience. You might think the truly mentally tough never want to quit, but the truth is that perseverance is usually about keeping going even though you really want to stop."

So how do you do that? How do you push on when you're at your lowest and just want to crawl away and hide from the world for a while? Reflecting on my experience and that of those with whom I have worked over the years, the first step is to make sure your life's purpose is clear and the goal(s) you have established are relevant, realistic, and time-bound. Additionally, make sure that each goal has one or more action steps that, once completed, can be measured and contribute to achieving the goal. The second step is to continue at a realistic pace and keep going.

Honestly, I faced the "perseverance issue" this morning as I do almost every other morning. I am an early to rise person who reads a number of devotions and has a light breakfast, and then I head to the gym with the intent of investing 45 minutes to one hour of my morning in working out. I begin with the upper body routines, followed by the elliptical and treadmill. Today about halfway through my time on the elliptical, my enthusiasm began to wane and as I looked to my left at the treadmill, I had the thought of passing on the opportunity to spend another grueling thirty minutes of punishment! That was when all the steps came to mind. I kept going because in my mind I could see myself finishing strong and experiencing the positive feeling that goes along with keeping my word to myself! And,

93. Churchill, Winston. "Never Give In, Never, Never, Never Never, 1941." National Churchill Museum. https://www.nationalchurchillmuseum.org/winston-churchill-speeches-1941-1946.html.

94. Stillman, Jessica. 5 Steps to Persevere (Even When You Really Want to Quit). Inc., November 25, 2015.

remembering the spirit of Ms. Stillman's words, I knew my efforts would pay off simply by putting one foot in front of the other for only a few more minutes—the most basic example of perseverance would lead me to a successful end!

———————

Fortunately, for the times, we started learning the proper application of each of the topics discussed above as we played with our little friends in the sandbox and refined as the years passed. Unfortunately, our current, "self-centered" society calls for a greater focus than we anticipated growing up. The "I-focused" individuals in our midst are skeptical and overly interested in themselves. As humble leaders who are interested in the advancement "all comers," we must focus on each area. For example, we must stand strongly in favor of diversity, inclusion, and tolerance in our institutions; we must recognize the adaptability and flexibility of our followers; we must encourage the flourishing of creativity and innovation; we must exhibit and respect healthy patriotism and citizenship; we must commit ourselves courageously to self-discipline, temperance, and stability; we must model critical thinking, strategic thinking, and problem solving for those who follow; and we must challenge ourselves to pursue ever higher levels of integrity. To be sure, this is a lot of "musts." Therefore, there will be a need for perseverance more than ever before; the "leadership hill" we are required to climb has grown tall and is not for the faint of heart.

APPLICATION QUESTIONS

- Why is a focus on diversity and inclusion so important?

- Considering the generally, self-centered nature of today's workforce, why is a focus on tolerance so important?

- Considering the "multinational characteristic" of much of the American workforce, share your thoughts on patriotism and citizenship.

- What role does self-discipline, temperance, and stability play in the leadership of others?

- Objective analysis and evaluation of an issue is important when forming good judgements. How may one become more proficient in critical thinking? Can strategic thinking be developed? If yes or no is your answer, explain why. What is the most important step in problem solving?

- Explain "integrity" and how you demonstrate this quality.

- How can one develop perseverance?

- Each of the above qualities is essential to humble leadership. In the event you fall short on one or more of these, what is your solution to the problem?

CHAPTER 10: Passionate Commitment to Action: *Difficult Behaviors that Reap Miracles*

Are you up to the challenge? We have already covered the core virtues and values that the humble leader prioritizes in his or her community. How does one identify the humble leader from his day-to-day behavior?

I have attempted to divide these qualities into two groups. The first group, which we detailed in Section II, is referred to as virtues, which are features of your character and provide the foundation of principle and good moral being. Considered humanistic in nature, they are understood as convictions, attitudes, or lifestyles centered on human interest or values. The second group includes the priorities and behaviors that can be incorporated into your daily routines by following straightforward guidelines, checklists, and rules; your ability to perform in these areas can be measured. Nevertheless, I believe it is the virtues and one's passion for others that constitute and directly enable the humble leader to perform well in these more tangible environments, and as such, it is my desire that you continue to meditate on the virtues from previous chapters as you consider these tangible behaviors and add action to your passions.

This chapter begins with detailing the basic components of communication in the leader's tool belt, such as listening, public speaking, writing, and small groups, and then progresses to using these interpersonal tools to develop engagement and empower others and share leadership. Next the chapter argues for an internal customer focus and explains how to create a shared vision within an institution and build partnerships outside one's institution. Lastly, the chapter details how to manage conflict and achieve conflict resolution and how to succeed in negotiating.

Personal and Interpersonal Competence

How well you know, understand, and employ your personal assets—mind, body, and spirit, and the extent to which you take personal responsibility for the results of your personal assets speak to your level of self-command. Your personal competence enables you to focus on the "big" picture and accept life as it comes, knowing that harmony in mind, body, and spirit give rise to a wholeness of life within which are the three aspects of a human's field of interest—truth, beauty, and goodness. The humble leader who demonstrates personal competence sets a standard for others to follow.

Interpersonal competence is evidence of your ability to employ these personal assets when connecting with others. When you exercise your ability to connect and establish a good relationship, you have realized a major milestone in your journey toward becoming a humble leader. Good interpersonal relations refer to the ability to communicate with and understand your team. It is the ability you use every day when you interact with other people, both individually and in groups, and is the ability made up of many components that come into play throughout a diverse range of scenarios. They include communication skills—listening, questioning, and observation of body language, as well as skills associated with emotional and social intelligence, such as the ability to persuade and influence, to manage conflict and change, and to encourage collaboration and cooperation.

It is the leader fueled by his or her passion for others that will excel at interpersonal relations. They are easily recognized as good listeners, who build strong relationships and are flexible and open-minded. They negotiate effectively, solicit performance feedback, and handle constructive criticism exceedingly well. They seek collaborative decisions and convey respect to those with whom disagree.

These skills are most important for an effective leader and we will break down a few of these components in the following pages. Furthermore, there are numerous books available to improve your knowledge in these areas ,and three that I have found to be very helpful are *Emotional Intelligence* by Daniel Goleman, *Social Intelligence* by Daniel Goleman and *Difficult Conversations* by Douglas Stone.

Communication

There are three primary types of communication: verbal, nonverbal, and written. Verbal communications consist of spoken words. Nonverbal communication consists of body language—the tone of voice, hand gestures and facial expressions, etc.—and written communications consist of written words. Each of these methods is useful to transmit information. Even though there are those who place greater value on one method versus another, I can't seem to find sufficient, verifiable data to support such a preference for every scenario. Rather I think it is important to let the content of one's message dictate the medium through which it is communicated— is this best delivered as a one on one conversation, a company-wide announcement, or an email?

Effective communications are often a challenge, and the continuously evolving world of technology certainly plays a role. There seems to have emerged a language that challenges even the most adept. Continuous advances in social media platforms require that the uninitiated remain alert to the new demands. Nevertheless, as these evolving requirements for effective communications continue to invade our culture, the old requirements seem to remain.

Kevin McSpadden published the following in *Time*[95] on May 14, 2015:

> The average attention span for the notoriously ill-focused goldfish is nine seconds, but according to a study completed by Microsoft Corp., people now generally lose concentration after *eight seconds,*

---

95. McSpadden, Kevin. "You Now Have a Shorter Attention Span Than a Goldfish." *Time.* May 14, 2015.

highlighting the effects of an increasingly digitized lifestyle on the brain.

Researchers in Canada surveyed 2,000 participants and studied the brain activity of 112 others using electroencephalograms (EEGs). Microsoft found that since the year 2000 (or about when the mobile revolution began) the average attention span dropped from 12 seconds to eight seconds.

"Heavy multi-screeners find it difficult to filter out irrelevant stimuli—they're more easily distracted by multiple streams of media," the report read.

On the positive side, the report says our ability to multitask has drastically improved in the mobile age.

Microsoft theorized that the changes were a result of the brain's ability to adapt and change itself over time and a weaker attention span may be a side effect of evolving to a mobile Internet.

Most have had the experience of being in a conversation in which both parties speak the same language, but what is being heard and what was intended to be communicated are worlds apart. Sometimes, when speaking about simple or complex matters of interest one can feel like they are walking across a broken bridge and believe they are speaking into a world going deaf. Considering this shortened attention span and the cacophony of sounds that emerge from a collection of new languages, is it any wonder that blank stares are the all too often response to the particulars of a unique vocabulary?

To communicate clearly, one must acknowledge that their background—the way they think and act—as well as the listener's background will shape their message, as language is critically affected by its setting and circumstances. Human vocabulary misunderstandings result from differences in experiences and ways of understanding those experiences. As citizens of a multicultural society, it is incumbent on each person to be aware of differences in cultures and the factors that have influenced these cultures—ethnicity, gender, religion, countries of origin, etc. It is crucial to maintain a high level of knowledge of these differences if communications are going to be successful.

I often share with others the thought that if you never leave your hometown your worldview will be characterized only by those early experiences, whether that be a life in the country, a city, or suburbia. Often, one's culture is reflective of their home environment and the way they communicate has emerged from that culture. Keep this in mind when you have the opportunity to study the art of communication and have the chance to communicate with someone from somewhere new!

With the above as background, rank yourself on a scale of 1 to 10 as a communicator based on the following:

1. I understand verbal, non-verbal, and written communications and use them appropriately.

2. I create accurate and punctual reports.

3. I effectively deliver well-prepared, interesting, and informative presentations.

4. I share information and ideas with others, and when decisions are made, I communicate them in a timely fashion to others.

5. I communicate in an open, authentic manner.

6. I attentively listen to others with understanding.

7. I encourage feedback and foster a non-punitive atmosphere in which people can be frank and candid.

It is doubtful that one naturally ranks high on each of the above parameters at all times. However, if we keep in mind that the end goal is to seek to understand the other person and establish a basis for presenting yourself in such a way that you will be understood, the results that follow will be worth the effort and those with whom you attempt to communicate will be grateful!

Listening

Listening is integral to effective communications, yet many of us are so busy formulating our comments while awaiting our opportunity to speak that we often miss what is being said. Listening, like weather reports, is often a subject about which a lot is said, but little is done. Make no mistake, however, the leader with good, active and intentional listening skills will always stand higher on the ladder of success than those who are less accomplished in this important area. Truly, good listeners often hold higher-level positions and are promoted more often than those with less effective listening skills. And, it is my observation that good institutions that make the transition from good to great are those made up of good listeners.

In an effort to be a good listener and avoid being the person who can hardly wait their turn to speak, the good listener will go deeper in a conversation by getting out of their own head and away from their perceptions, biases, and ideas. Rather than being the person who is busy preparing what they intend to say when given the chance, they place their interests in the background and carefully observe the speaker to pick up on mannerisms that communicate beyond their spoken words. They maintain good eye-contact to demonstrate interest and ask clarifying questions to make certain what is being said is understood. Some may find that they can become consumed by the pressure to formulate and voice their own thoughts that they completely zone out of the discussion happening around them. If this is an area you struggle with, you may benefit from making a more concentrated effort to contemplate the issues or material to be discussed in advance and journaling your thoughts. While not always feasible, it will ease your anxiety to have those thoughts "saved" and help you be "in the moment."

There are a variety of sources available via the internet that you may find very useful when working on "active, intentional listening skills." Following are a few useful pointers I found:

1. Show that you are truly interested by your questions, maintaining eye contact and other body language. Show that you are listening with a smile (or other appropriate facial expressions) and posture (when appropriate, a slight leaning toward your speaker shows interest).

2. Maintain attention and avoid distractions. It's easy to be distracted when a bird flies by, a phone rings, or a door slams. Good eye contact helps avoid this problem.

3. Be patient and respond occasionally to the speaker indicating you see things from his or her point of view.

In group settings, the humble leader proficient in listening will also be able to observe the participants who aren't actively speaking, and when appropriate will use their "moment to speak" as it were to draw the quiet ones into the conversation and encourage them to elicit their thoughts.

Public Speaking

Billionaire Warren Buffett says that public speaking is the most valuable skill you can learn, boosting your career value by 50%![96] I devoted a great deal of time and effort to this area and did well during my career. Did my public speaking skills contribute 50% to my value? I don't actually know. I do know that it built personal confidence, improved my communication skills, gave me useful insights into group dynamics and helped me gain a more accurate and deeper intuitive understanding of other people.

For the humble leader, comfort with public speaking is a very important asset but may not be necessary. There have been very effective, successful leaders who were not considered outstanding public speakers (I prefer not to name names), yet led their institutions to high levels of success. Without question, the ability to present information to a live audience of any size provides the opportunity to inform, persuade, and entertain. How-

---

96. Gallo, Carmine. "The One Skill Warren Buffett Says Will Raise Your Value By 50%." *Inc. Magazine.* Jan 5, 2017. https://www.inc.com/carmine-gallo/the-one-skill-warren-buffett-says-will-raise-your-value-by-50.html.

ever, I limit my enthusiasm for public speaking as a method for *inform-ing* and *persuading* because an audience's attention span is quite short and often falls prey to distractions. These two factors interfere with complete information transfer, thus interfering with the "persuasion" process. As for entertainment, public speaking can be very useful. For example, an enter-taining speech, delivered by a well-informed speaker may open the door for individual or small group discussions where transfer of information can take place and increase the likelihood of persuasion.

The ability to speak well to a public audience is another arrow in the hum-ble leader's quiver. Following are a few suggestions you will find useful:

1. Become a student of your message—know your "stuff."

2. Pay careful attention to other speakers. What do they do well and not so well? What would you do differently?

3. Join Toastmasters International. Chapters are ubiquitous, they are easy to join, the cost is low, and will provide essentially all you need to become a good speaker.

4. Seek opportunities to speak. The more you speak, the better you become.

5. Encourage criticism. You will learn the value of this in Toastmasters.

Writing

Social media being what it is today, you may not be receptive to me stress-ing the importance of quality writing skills. However, I continue to stick to my guns; sound bites and abbreviated words may have their place but can never promise the clarity and winsomeness of good writing. Well-writ-ten documents continue to inform, persuade, and entertain, as does the spoken word, and uniquely allow and often require a greater degree of intention and specificity. If you are a clear and effective writer, you can use this to your advantage to communicate in greater detail and concreteness, and additionally, you can often avoid the all too common dilemma of "he said, she said."

A few things the humble leader may ask themselves concerning their writing skills would be:

1. Can I explain the logic of an idea in a succinct way?

2. Do I understand how to use correct grammar, punctuation, and spelling?

3. Does it sound correct when I read it aloud? When someone else reads it aloud?

4. Why am I writing this?

5. Do I know the audience for whom I am writing?

There is much more to be said about writing skills so let me leave the subject by suggesting that the humble leader will measure much of his or her success by their ability to effectively communicate. As said earlier, communications allow information transfer, persuasion, and entertainment, which always present daily challenges.

Technologically Savvy

In the recent past, it was acceptable to turn to the younger person in your "shop" and say, "You're better at this (computer, smart phone, etc.) than I so take care of it!" No more! The need for high-tech ability is here to stay. To underscore my point, the term, "tech-savvy" appears in the current *English Oxford Living Dictionary* and is defined as, "well informed about or proficient in the use of modern technology, especially computers." While it may be unrealistic to set for yourself the goal of becoming a technological expert, you must be proficient enough to be able to ask the right questions, understand the answer, and add new skills. How do you measure up?

The humble leader who commands the respect of all audiences:

1. Strives to acquire the technical knowledge needed to succeed in today's and tomorrow's world.

2. Knows the technological needs for the institution and successfully recruits people with needed technological expertise.

3. Effectively manages the issue of technology to increase productivity.

Small Groups

Once you have understood the above necessary components of communication, an excellent arena to put these skills into practice and see them come to life is the small group. A small group of four to five people is the ideal tool for engaging individuals within a community, creating broader fields of understanding, and ultimately changing the culture. The necessary first step is to connect, get to know, and establish relationships with members of the community. In the appendix, you will find my full report of the Small Group Initiative for the University of Maryland, School of Dentistry, which will give you a real life example of the outcome of such a focus within an institution. You will also find tips for designing your own program, selecting participants, establishing a meeting schedule, formulating the meeting agenda, and so forth.

Engage Your Followers

You will remember from the Introduction that Gallup's research revealed that only 13% of employees around the world are actively engaged at work, and in the United States, that number is in the neighborhood of 30-31%. More than $350 billion has been invested in leadership development worldwide without solving the frightening lack of workforce engagement. How does the humble leader actively combat this widespread disengagement?

I truly believe the adage: "Once you have found the job you love; you will never work a day in your life." You will be engaged! You will never be overwhelmed! You will never work too hard! The question is, "Where are those jobs?" The answer is, "They are where there are humble leaders." Humble leaders encourage you to develop your seeds of greatness. They encourage your mind to transcend perceived limitations. They encourage your consciousness to expand in every direction and find new, great and wonderful worlds. It is the humble leaders who give life to a job with which you can fall in love, enjoy the fruits of your labor and never work a day in your life! Humble leaders affect an institution's culture from its roots, and provide the soil for everyone to realize their hopes and dreams.

The late Steve Jobs said to the Stanford Graduating Class of 2005, "Your work is going to fill a large part of your life, and the only way to be truly satisfied is to do what you believe is great work. And the only way to do great work is to love what you do. If you haven't found it yet, keep looking."[97] Patanjali, who was a sage in India to whom several important ancient Sanskrit works are ascribed, offered a similar view when he wrote, "When you are inspired by some great purpose, some extraordinary project, all your thoughts break their bounds. Your mind transcends limitations, your consciousness expands in every direction, and you find yourself in a new, great and wonderful world. Dormant forces, faculties, and talents become alive, and you discover yourself to be a greater person by far than you ever dreamed yourself to be."[98]

The engaged individuals can be recognized in their personal life as well as their professional life. In their personal lives, they are fully absorbed by and enthusiastic about the people with whom they interact each day. They take positive action to establish and further relationships. They get to know others quite well and become well acquainted with their essential aspects: their values, aspirations, educational and employment backgrounds, family, etc. In their professional lives, the engaged employees bring to the job the same level of investment. They are passionate about the job and voluntarily invest time and effort above and beyond that which is required for individual performance. Additionally, the engaged employees recognize themselves as leaders. They know that others are always watching and often emulating their behavior. They assume full responsibility for modeling a "humble leadership pace." This is a pace that sets exceptionally high standards of performance and calls for everyone to fulfill tasks with better attention to

97. Jobs, Steve. "Stanford Commencement Address." Stanford, June 14, 2005 https://news.stanford.edu/2005/06/14/jobs-061505/.

98. Patanjali. Goodreads. https://www.goodreads.com/quotes/358433-when-you-are-inspired-by-some-great-purpose-some-extraordinary.

detail and proficiency, without undercutting morale and making people feel as though they are failing. This pace promotes the right conditions for all members of that institution to give their best each day, to be committed to their institution's goals and values, motivated to contribute to institutional success, and enjoy a sense of their own well-being.

The humble leader recognizes his or her responsibility to enhance employee engagement, thus changing a community's culture to create an environment that supports the flourishing of others. This culture shift can be achieved, but the humble leader must realize that 1) change must be initiated immediately, as it is human nature to become a part of the culture we inhabit; 2) this change happens slowly, sometimes as the product of years of intentionality, and it is a never ending process; 3) metrics must be established for one to be able to evaluate the desired changes.

Is Your Work a Calling?

When we enter the workforce, we often do so with the idea of earning enough money to pay our bills and, as time goes on, bills for our family. A good job or career usually does that, but all too often it can make one feel trapped in an apparent endeavor that seems to have no end and one we do not particularly enjoy or connect with on any level. In contrast, a calling is something that may have begun in early life as a tiny thought or feeling, which began to consume our mind and drive us to an imagined end. In many cases this imagined end is the "big picture," which is the result of our anticipated efforts. This picture reveals and captivates us with all that is true, good, and beautiful, and we can experience great pleasure while pursuing our chosen vocation. Even though we may be performing the same tasks as the person who feels trapped, our attitude is different and sure enough it isn't work to us! Some of us are fortunate enough to "feel" this calling early in life and jobs, careers, and opportunities seem to just fall into place. For others of us, our relationship with a humble leader may spark this feeling of a calling, as they encourage us to refine our abilities.

A story is told that when the late President John Kennedy was visiting NASA, he asked an engaged janitor what he was doing, the janitor replied, "I'm helping to put a man on the Moon."

A similar story I heard on this topic was about three bricklayers. An interested bystander asked the first man what he was doing, and the man said he was laying bricks. After asking the second man the same question, he said he was putting up a wall. After asking the third man what he was doing, he answered, "I'm building a cathedral."

One man was laying bricks; he had a job. Another man was building a cathedral; he had a calling. One man was tightening bolts on a rocket booster—he had a job. Another man was helping put a man on the moon. He had a calling.

Do you look at what you do every day as a calling?

This is a far reaching question and one that you will need to keep refining throughout life, and there may not be one singular calling. I have difficulty imagining a purpose that would not benefit from one acting as the humble leader, and what is more, in this capacity, you will be uniquely equipped to aid others in refining their purpose. My daughter, who is more than 50 years young, chose a second career and graduated from the University of Maryland's School of Nursing this past December. After successfully completing requirements for a double major a few years ago and raising a family, she recognized a broader use for her degree, a further refinement of what she believed she was meant to do. While your current chosen track may not necessarily be the one of your dreams, if you are able to hold space for the bigger picture, you will see how this present "calling" enables you to make a difference in mankind's well-being. In other words, you may be 'laying bricks' today, but as you envision the 'cathedral,' and move forward with intent and passion, you will be living life as it was intended to be lived and able to contribute to the flourishing of others in more effective ways!

People Development and Empowerment

The leader seriously engaged in people development and empowerment demonstrates a consistent and voluble respect for others and keeps a keen eye out for areas where a gift or adeptness can be further refined as well as areas that are ignored, undeveloped, or unrecognized as important. The empowered employee is the engaged employee. They take possession of the institution's aims, exercise full responsibility for their personal performance, and are an inspiration to others. You can count on them to help co-workers, teammates and collaborators see their unique value and strengths. Not everyone will welcome further development or be interested in continuing what should be a life-long education process; the humble leader will creatively and winsomely attempt to engage these individuals, whether it be through small groups or a development of a one on one relationship.

If I may digress, I will share a story of a personal experience that made a profound impression on me—it is an impression that has served me exceedingly well throughout my life.

I was sitting on a sofa, across the desk from Malcolm Rogers (manager of the Miami Sales Area Office at Upjohn). I was there for the sole purpose of his naming me to my first level management position—Manager, North Florida District, to be based in Jacksonville, Florida. Following a few congratulatory comments, Malcolm looked across his desk to me and said the following: "Hal, I want you to imagine that between my hands is a huge pile of manila rope. As you 'see' me slide this rope across this desk to you, I ask you to take it with the assurance that it is yours to assist in your growing as high in your career as you would like to grow. Remember always, I am here to be of help in any way I can and am committed to that effort. If, for some reason, you happen to fall, I am here to catch you." These words, steeped in the passion he had for my own flourishing, were the perfect "send-off," and they were truly instrumental in my reaching a top position in The Upjohn Company!

Another story came about as a result of a conversation I had with Dr. Perman, when I brought up the subject I'm writing about here. Knowing his leadership style well enough, and that he maintained a genuine focus in the development of others, I asked: "Of the many people you have worked with over the years, do many of them have the view of development you have?"

His answer: "It's mixed. I would say, regrettably, that in this [the University] or any other setting, the majority of people that I know are selfish. They're inwardly directed and not outwardly directed. It's all about them before it's about anybody else. And this brings me to another related point. I have found as I've evolved as a leader, and this comes back to the humility thing and I think I'm being genuine in saying this, I'm highly responsible here and don't have to tell anyone. I find, as I watch people evolve or look at people in their leadership positions, they too often feel they need to remind people that they're the leader, that they're the boss. To the ones that will take counsel from me, I tell them that what I've learned is that if you are truly a special leader, you never need to bring it up, everybody else will do the talking for you."

Toward the end of a similar conversation with Dr. Cole at MUSC, he referred me to a quote from Lao Tzu, an ancient Chinese Philosopher with whose philosophy he agreed, and was the author of the Tao Te Ching. As an aside, Tao Te Ching is the central Taoist text and was apparently written as a guide for rulers. It defined the Tao, or way, and established the philosophical basis of Taoism, which advocates humility and religious piety. In this text, we read that: "A leader is best when people barely know he exists. When his work is done, his aim fulfilled, and they will say: 'We did it ourselves.'"

Both Dr. Perman and Dr. Cole recognized that everyone is a leader, whether they were the boss or not, and that those who prioritize the goal of developing and empowering others never need to announce their position in the hierarchy to achieve acclaim!

The humble leader who is truly interested in developing and empowering others:

1. Consistently treats people with dignity and considers the needs, feelings and concerns of others.

2. Asks people what they need to do their work better and ensures that they receive the training they need to succeed. Furthermore, this leader provides effective coaching and developmental feedback in a timely manner.

3. Takes on a mentoring role when appropriate, challenges others with the aim of their continued development, and helps them build confidence by helping them visualize success.

4. Gives people the freedom they need to do their job well, even if this requires taking risks in trusting others to make decisions and avoiding micromanagement, knowing full well that you are ultimately responsible for the decision that has been made.

5. Provides personal, genuine recognition for others' achievements and rewards hard work and risk-taking.

6. Accepts mistakes with grace and turns them into learning experiences.

7. Provides clear tangible opportunities for growth and development.

8. Effectively helps people focus on a common purpose.

Share Leadership

The humble leader is unique, and the humble leader who shares leadership well is a diamond in the rough. Shared leadership distributes leadership responsibility in such a way that employees within the organization lead each other. This shared leadership responsibility is not without risk but it truly gives life to the statement, "Everyone is a leader!" Therefore, in addition to knowing the followers and their abilities well, a humble leader must develop and maintain relationships with each individual that encourages them to perform at a high level and in concert with the organization's goals. Knowing that the employee has the aptitude and commitment to excellent performance provides the humble leader with a foundation for minimizing risk, supporting self-confidence and embracing a true, courageous commitment to others.

The humble leader focused on sharing leadership:

1. Willingly delegates his or her responsibilities to the institution's employees.

2. Defers to others when they have more expertise.

3. Strives to arrive at an outcome *with* others rather than *for* others, whether they are in a leadership or follower role.

4. Creates an environment where people focus on the larger good and avoids sub-optimization or "turfism."

5. Develops a relationship of mutual respect, trust, and responsibility with colleagues.

6. Seeks collaborative decisions and conveys respect to those who disagree.

The investment demanded of the humble leader when he or she prioritizes the development and empowerment of others and chooses to share leadership is not slight. If you try to create the strong organization we are pursuing by making daily habits of each of the bullet points in this section, you will realize you have taken on a major task. Let your passion for the individuals in your organization be your fuel and remember others may look back and identify you as the leader Malcolm Rogers was for me.

Internal Customer Focus

There is an old saying, nothing happens until someone sells something. This is true whether you are selling tomatoes on the street corner or ideas within an institution. This being true, it holds that there are customers on the street corner, as well as inside the institution. Even though they may not always be right, the employees of an institution will always be buying and selling within its doors, and thus, their worries, wishes and working conditions must be addressed.

The term, customer focus, is usually indicative of the buying and selling process, is associated with suppliers and [external] consumers in the wholesale and retail settings, and does not always include those serving or being served within the institution. The humble leader recognizes his or her followers, the institution's employees, as customers and treats them accordingly!

If we assume the "customer is always right" point of view and there comes a situation where a customer's desires or demands of a company do not synchronize with the company's goals, then it becomes the humble leader's "mission" to establish a relationship that provides an opportunity to share information and establish a dialogue of some form between both parties. If you happen to be at or near the top of the hierarchy in a "for-profit" or "not-for-profit" institution and fail to see fellow workers in the same light as you see your [external] customers, then you will likely fall into the trap of neglecting their input and not bothering to dialogue with them concerning the institution's goals. In other words, they will not be seen as important customers but only as employees whose job is to do what is expected without question. They are not seen as an "important customer" but one whose job and responsibility is to perform according to the standards set forth by the boss. This is the wrong assumption, as the internal customer is just as important (possibly more so) as the external customer. They require the same respect since their attitude toward customers is a reflection of the respect leadership shows them. The humble leader's duty is to ensure that internal customers are a focus of the institution; furthermore, the humble leader may be the best builder of internal and external customer loyalty by setting the example for others to follow.

Based on the reality that every employee is a leader, the employee's focus on fellow employees is important, whether the institution is small or large. Filled with this leadership calling, the employee enhances internal customer satisfaction by soliciting opinions and ideas from them, solving problems and in collaboration, sets achievable customer expectations. He or she responds to all internal customers' needs where possible and ensures that commitments to fellow employees are met.

There is essentially no end to the importance of focusing on fellow employees and the extent to which employees conduct themselves in the workplace. This is a measure of the humble leader's influence. A serious interest really is reflective of the passion we hold for the "person next door" and improves engagement and adds satisfying value to every employee's experience. Prioritizing this in your leadership will result in a strong team that is committed to each other and performs with an understanding and acceptance of the institution's purpose, vision, values, and goals. Following the humble leader's example, relationships of mutual influence ensue that build confidence and encourage assumption of personal responsibility for all things within the employee's area of responsibility. An assessment of the humble leader's performance always includes a focus on internal customers.

Create a Shared Vision

A shared vision is vital when building an organization where employees are engaged in their job. This can be a time-consuming experience, but once completed, the vision enhances focus, energizes, and inspires the pursuit of things that are important to the workforce.

The first step in this process is to communicate to the organization the parameters in which the vision will be established (ie. the present day resources at its disposal—space, employees, financial capabilities, etc). This avoids wide-ranging discussions that are not necessarily relevant to the task, and permits all involved to understand the priorities, known limits, and variables to be considered when defining the future state. With the parameters established and clearly understood by all participants, the question is asked, "What do we want our institution to look like in five years?" Once the vision is established, the leader facilitates discussions that give rise to a strategic plan.

The strategic plan begins with developing the purpose statement, a statement that asks, "Why do we come to work each day?" Next is the development of goals that are specific, measurable, achievable, realistic and time-bound. Each goal is followed by strategic and tactical steps that, when implemented, move the institution toward its goals. Finally, required resources are identified and steps for measuring progress are established.

To be sure, developing a shared vision and strategic plan are major efforts because they encourage input from as many employees as possible and the effort requires plenteous patience on the part of the leader. Once completed, however, the endeavor inspires people to stretch their thinking and contribute to following the plan, and become more engaged in their job. As the humble leader initiates a method of communicating encouraging messages of progress, he or she will have a very productive workforce.

Build Partnerships

Practitioners of the leadership process are committed to building partnerships. They understand the value, "two minds are better than one" and strongly encourage unification of people. They treat coworkers as partners, not competitors. They unite the organization into a proficient team. They build effective partnerships across the institution and are considered a source of inspiration. They are a positive influence in that their manner of doing things discourages destructive comments about other people or groups. Furthermore, they build effective alliances with other organizations inside and outside of their institution by taking personal responsibility for all that happens in their sphere of influence and showing respect to the missions of others.

Leaders who exhibit this strength think long term to create a network of relationships that help get things done and where parties agree to cooperate to advance their mutual interests. They understand that pursuing outcomes that achieve each party's mission only adds to success and amplifies a community's reach.

Managing Conflict & Behavior

Disagreements are healthy, make life interesting, and often are the soil of new improvements; however this is only true if the disagreements between individuals are expressed with respect for each other and motivated by the ultimate good of the entire institution. We would like to think that the likes of good manners and getting along with others were things we all learned in the sandbox. But, if you place any credence in the "Jekyll—Hyde" story described at the beginning of this work, you know that many of us didn't and you know why! It was reported in The RAND Blog that "frequent hostility and rising inequality are only two of a wide array of challenges Americans face in the workplace."[99] Economist Kathleen Mullen highlighted findings from the recently released *RAND American Working Conditions Survey*, which suggested that "one out of five American workers report some type of hostility (on the job)—whether it's bullying, harassment, and even violence in the workplace."[100] All too often, disagreements trigger personal wound to our egos and become instruments of destruction within the community. Managing conflict is and always will be a major challenge and opportunity for the humble leader to deal with conflicts without hesitation.

Conflicts come in all sizes and shapes: salaries ("That person makes more than me, and my job requires just as much effort!"); promotions ("I've been here longer—why didn't I get the job?"); recognition ("Everyone gets noticed but me!" or "I'm being micromanaged!" or "The boss never gives me the *new* opportunities!"). The list is endless.

It is generally accepted that business management began in the United States in the late 1800s and what we would recognize as leadership of an institution has been in existence since the late 1700s. These years would be included in what we refer to as the modern era and many would assume

99. Roback, Warren. "Exploring the Challenges Facing American Workers." The RAND Blog. September 15, 2017 https://www.rand.org/blog/2017/09/exploring-the-challenges-facing-american-workers.html.

100. Roback, Warren. "Exploring the Challenges Facing American Workers." The RAND Blog. September 15, 2017 https://www.rand.org/blog/2017/09/exploring-the-challenges-facing-american-workers.html.

that conflict within an institution began around the same time period. Such is not the case. Suggested methods for resolving conflicts were recorded during Biblical times and the following method was lifted directly from the Book of Matthew.

> If another believer sins against you, go privately and point out the offense. If the other person listens and confesses it, you have won that person back. But if you are unsuccessful, take one or two others with you and go back again, so that everything you say may be confirmed by two or three witnesses. If the person still refuses to listen, take your case to the church.[101]

Based on my experience, individuals involved in a conflict or confrontation are rarely happy that it has emerged and would be very pleased if it would simply go away. However, these situations almost never diffuse on their own and often fester. Someone has been rendered helpless or emotionally wounded, whether intentionally or unintentionally, and must go through a healing process. Depending on the individual, the victim may demand a "pound of flesh," which is another way of saying that the assumed perpetrator must be punished. Without question, conflicts can be serious and become extremely complex very quickly as the two or more sides clarify and become firmly planted in their positions. However, if neglected, they begin to "smolder," go underground and become a constant, often unrecognized negative force of influence for years to come. Therefore, it is necessary that the humble leader makes every effort to learn about and understand the details of the conflict, and then take appropriate steps as soon as possible to resolve the issue(s). While this is not an easy process, no one other than the humble leader should take responsibility for the reconciliation of their followers and unity of their institution; the outcome of this very process rests on your shoulders and the duty should not be passed off to others. As mentioned earlier, I have found that applying my interpretation of the principles set forth in Matthew 18 to be useful.

---

101. Matthew 18:15-17, NLT.

The *first step* is to meet with each opposing party individually for the sole purpose of demonstrating understanding and respect for the party's position and establishing a working relationship. I typically strive to meet with the "injured" party first and ask whether they trust that I understand the details of the matter. If they do not have this trust in me, I make time for a one on one meeting with them to hear their side. The meeting is strictly confidential, and absent a "threatening atmosphere"; total honesty is encouraged. During this discussion, I will carefully listen and attempt to identify points where agreement between both parties is possible, and make a written or mental note of these points and consider using them at the next meeting if a next meeting is necessary. Furthermore, I will set the expectation that I will be hearing both parties' "sides of the story" and that re-unification is my ultimate goal, so as to avoid any misunderstandings or feelings of betrayal. Once they feel heard, I will make the same effort to hear the "perpetrator's" side in a private, confidential, non-threatening atmosphere, always with an eye to points that will unify the two parties. Additionally, if it is determined during discussions with either party that our institution's policies have played a role in the altercation and require reform, I will communicate that I am taking that under advisement as well and will be working to make the environment less threatening and more supportive to its members. If a good sense of understanding and trust emerges among all members involved, a thorough discussion of the issues may take place between the two parties.

The *second step*, assuming there is one, is to encourage a discussion of positions held; I will begin this meeting by stating the goal of the reconciliation effort—all parties involved need to make sure their position is based on accurate information, take full responsibility for their position, and respect that the other party has done the same thing. Then it will be necessary that the parties in error (and this may include the institution as well) are willing to yield and change the destructive behavior. It is important that the humble leader takes an active part and directs the conversation to the previously noted points of common understanding and the biggest issues at hand, so this meeting does not become a full rehash from both sides. This discussion may be a difficult and time-consuming step since factors such as cultural differences, highly emotional individuals, and language barriers make it difficult to reach a mutual understanding. Persistence and focus often pay off, however, so keep the discussion going. Experience has shown that weak, less serious or significant points of contention will tend to disappear in the face of open discussion. When the critical issues are clearly recognized by both parties, the opportunity for compromise can be identified.

During this step, keep in mind that when you have brought both parties together to the point of compromise and closure, there may remain a few open wounds and a few, short side-meetings may be necessary for those who feel a need to appeal their case, to be heard one more time if necessary. For parties bearing the majority of the weight of the compromise, these side meetings communicate that the leader recognizes their sacrifice, truly cares, and can go a long way to speeding the healing process. Furthermore, the humble leader can reframe the outcome of the discussion in a positive light such that it is understood that while no single individual received all that they wanted, the end result will be for the betterment of the institution.

Unfortunately, there will be instances, rare in my experience, when the above doesn't work. There will be one or more individuals unwilling to reconcile and will therefore no longer be conducive to the institution's efforts in their previous environment. The humble leader shows their true colors when they go the extra mile to try to help the unwilling party find another community or occupation that better aligns with the individual's personal goals.

Throughout the above process, the humble leader takes the high road. He or she will have utilized good communication skills—listening well, understanding the issues, and providing sound input when appropriate. Additionally, he or she will have employed good interpersonal skills, showing respect for others, taking responsibility for the outcome, and encouraging others to do the same.

In the end, all people involved in the process become serious students of humanity, and specifically their followers, difficult and otherwise. They have become more clearly focused on what really matters, more respectful of the seriousness of the issues or conflicts, and have exercised dignity in expressions and attitudes as they achieve successful resolutions.

Negotiations

Humble leaders negotiate in an effort to settle differences and reach a compromise or an agreement so that all parties achieve the best possible outcome for their position or that of the organization they represent. The goal for good negotiations is, via the principles of fairness, that there are mutual benefits for all and good relationships are maintained.

A few years ago, I had the pleasure of a conversation with Dr. Lisa K. Saladin, Vice President for Academic Affairs and Provost at the Medical University of South Carolina. During our time together, I asked about negotiation skills as they may apply in the academic setting and whether these skills could be learned.

Her response was: "I've been in multiple situations; I actually teach some negotiation skills. Negotiating skills, you can teach it in a workshop; there are certain skill sets that you can learn related to negotiating that are sometimes basic to some individuals but for people that have never thought about it there is a great deal to know. If you're going to negotiate, you need to come to the table with an understanding of the players at the table and what they're probably interested in getting out of the situation. You need to do homework; you need to get some background information on the people that you're meeting with. You need to go in with an idea of what you're willing to give up and what you're not willing to give up. There are basic principles of negotiating that, I think, can be taught. It doesn't mean you're going to be good at them because you know the basic skill sets but once you know the basic skill sets and practice them, you can get better at them."

One of my follow-up questions had to do with the "willingness to give up" and whether that varies once one gets into negotiations or if it was fixed. Her reply was: "It depends. I've been in negotiating situations where on behalf of my professional association, we've been in legislative conflicts with other professions over some important language in practice acts, that is professional practice acts. As president of your association, you represent your membership, and if your membership says there is absolutely no way we will give up on this principle, you don't give up on that principle. It depends on whether you're negotiating as an individual or a representative of a group and then, who has the authority to make that final decision. In that heat of the moment, you would not negotiate that point. You might go back to membership and say if we don't move here, we're going to lose this but if that point is still absolutely no, then you're not going to be able to compromise. Other times, you actually have wiggle room and you know what range you have or what you're willing to compromise as you walk into that situation."

"Thinking about those things in advance—what are the potential opportunities, what are the potential consequences, who am I dealing with, what do they want, who stands to gain or lose the most in this negotiation—is extremely important. If you don't think about those things going in you do yourself harm in any negotiating situation. I think there are basic principles that can be taught and learned related to negotiating better."

Reflecting on the above, Dr. Saladin's advice is sound and applies to academia, business, religion, as well as other institutions. The humble leader will remember that there's always two sides to a negotiation and while we may well tend to focus on sacrificing as little as possible to achieve our own ends, it's sometimes good to yield on that highly focused position and develop a greater understanding of the win-win experience. To that end, that may mean we may make a greater investment than we anticipated, but we may also get a greater return.

As suggested at the beginning of this section, humble leaders accomplished at negotiations help us to settle differences. Those who are good at this process are able to find a middle ground and reach agreements where "win-win" results for all concerned emerge. They know how to handle conflicts so that serious disagreements are avoided. They approach the effort in a positive manner as they articulate their goals and recognize those of the other side. They maintain a high degree of fairness, seek value for all parties involved, and end with relationships that are willing to repeat the process if or when a new opportunity presents.

You may find the following points useful as you prepare to engage in this important process:

1. **Goals**—be clear on what you must achieve and try to anticipate the goal of the opposing party as well

2. **Non-negotiables**—be clear in your own mind as to the limits beyond which you will not negotiate and assume the opposing party has their own boundaries

3. **Be prepared**—learn as much as possible about the opposing negotiators and the institution they represent.

4. **Discussions**—Keep the discussion going with a question to the opposition. Silence can provide opportunities for negative positions to emerge, but the humble leader will seize the opportunity in these silences to genuinely inquire if the opposition is on the same page thus far. Accept the fact that a negative comment is an opportunity to pursue a positive "come back" so prepare accordingly.

5. **The Win-win**—maintain a focus on a positive outcome for all parties.

6. **Agreement is a Conclusion**—Stop the process when an agreement has been reached!

7. **Pursue Action**—Once the agreement has been reached, who does what next?

In Conclusion

I titled this chapter "Passionate Commitment to Action" because it is our passion for the individuals in our community and their flourishing that should motivate us to not only become adept listeners, vision creators, negotiators and so forth, but to put it into practice daily for their benefit. Since the humble leader will face issues related to each of the above topics, it is necessary that this leader plays an active role in each of these situations and refines his or her ability to employ effective techniques when called on to resolve problems as they occur within an institution. As the leader in your community and institution, it is your responsibility to prioritize, study, and continually develop these skills to the point that you can put them into practice at a moment's notice, as well as train the next generation of leaders who will have the same responsibility as they carry the organization into the future.

APPLICATION QUESTIONS:

- Explain how you may employ your personal assets—mind, body, spirit—in practical ways when establishing a humble leadership relationship.

- What are the problems inherent in verbal, nonverbal, and written communications and how can we utilize these mediums to bring clarity to the communication process? How would you go about improving your skills as a public speaker?

- Do you know what your purpose or calling is and has your vision of it refined through the years?

- What are practical ways you can contribute to employee engagement? How have you yourself been empowered by leadership in the past and what can you do to develop and empower others and why do you think it is important?

- Explain why you think a focus on "internal customers" is important.

- What, in your opinion, is the first and most important step in managing conflict, and why?

- What do you do when negotiations break down?

CHAPTER 11: What Makes Change Possible?

Throughout the previous 10 chapters, I have sought to describe the virtues and behaviors of the ideal, humble leader. I now include the adjective "ideal," as I recognize that it is unlikely that one individual lives out this description fully each day, and definitely not without serious conscious effort. Nevertheless, I do not desire to encourage complacency, as I know that it is possible for each of us to foster new virtues, set new priorities, and develop new skills. If you have felt overwhelmed or inadequate while reading the previous chapters, then this chapter is for you. Here I seek to persuade you with science that these changes to character are possible, and it is my desire to instill within you the hope, know-how and determination to be 1% better each day.

Where Social and Biological Sciences Meet

Even though much of a person's future is shaped during their early, formative years, one's future is not necessarily "set in stone." There is evidence that adult neurons can change their firing patterns and responses when faced with new experiences. While it was assumed at one time that what is referred to as neural plasticity settles down by adulthood, such is not the case. This finding, along with the advent of fields of study (e.g., positive psychology with its focus on personal growth) the need for encouraging humble leadership as defined earlier becomes even more clear.

Elsewhere in this book, I discussed trust and proposed that damaged trust, as with other human abilities, can be repaired or improved. The repair of trust may begin as soon as one overcomes what we commonly know as "confirmation bias"—the tendency to search for or interpret information in a way that confirms one's beliefs or impressions. Unquestionably, one must overcome the "fixed mindset," which interferes with learning and assume the possibility for change—improvement. There are those today who argue convincingly that one can actually change his or her DNA. If we can change our DNA, it is probably safe to assume we can change any element of our character. To illustrate this point, consider the following findings.

Robert Schneider, M.D., F.A.C.C., is a physician, scientist, educator, and one of the world's leading authorities on scientifically based, natural approaches for heart disease, high blood pressure, stress, and other cardiovascular risk factors. He did his postgraduate training in Internal Medicine at the University of Michigan Medical School. Over the past twenty years, he has directed nearly $20 million in research grants from the National Institutes of Health for his pioneering research on the natural approach to managing heart disease. The results of this groundbreaking research have been published in more than one hundred articles in authoritative medical journals and proceedings and featured in more than a thousand television, radio, magazine, and newspaper reports. In a lecture entitled "Mind Over DNA: Transforming DNA from the Inside Out (Our Conscious Future)," made available via YouTube, he opened with:

> The cutting of modern medicine is coming to the place where mind meets body, where mind meets DNA, where we have control over DNA, where we can control our genes from the inside out. This development of modern medicine very much parallels the science of meditation and its description and technologies for developing the mind-body connection... your DNA is not your destiny...![102]

Bruce Lipton, Ph. D., a cellular physiologist, argues similarly in his book *The Biology of Belief: Unleashing the Power of Consciousness, Matter and Miracles* for the mind-body connection:

---

102. Schneider, Robert. "Mind Over DNA: Transforming DNA from the Inside Out (Our Conscious Future)." May 13, 2014. https://www.youtube.com/watch?v=Gu33jzWYxQU.

Each of our cells is a living entity, and the main thing that influences them is our blood. If I open my eyes in the morning and my beautiful partner is in front of me, my perception causes a release of oxytocin, dopamine, growth hormones—all of which encourage the growth and health of my cells. But if I see a saber-toothed tiger, I'm going to release stress hormones, which change the cells to a protection mode. People need to realize that their thoughts are more primary than their genes, because the environment, which is influenced by our thoughts, controls the genes.[103]

Based on my understanding of his work, your perception determines the chemistry of your body, which elevates the power of the mind. Lipton's research and Schneider's findings regarding the mind-body relationship and changing DNA are compelling. This should encourage one to believe that if he or she can make up their mind to change their DNA, or any other complex system in the human body, one can certainly improve their trustworthiness or any other trait or virtue if there is thoughtful determination to do so.

Throughout these discussions of our ability to change ourselves, you might have noted that I repeatedly mention trust as an area for improvement because when the bond of trust is broken, many will say it cannot be repaired. Similarly, it is often said that one cannot change his or her DNA, but I've striven to show you that this is in fact possible. To be sure, within you are the genes (DNA) that bring forth extraordinary intellectual and creative power that can give rise to instincts. In the words of many positive thinkers, or "motivational individuals," these are the "seeds of greatness." Once this extraordinary intellectual and creative power is recognized and developed, it will deliver a level of performance that extends beyond one's imagination. This should encourage you to pick one of the qualities you wish to change or improve, make a commitment to yourself and others that you will practice that quality every day for at least 30 days. If you keep

---

103. Lipton, Bruce. *The Biology of Belief: Unleashing the Power of Consciousness, Matter and Miracles.* Carlsbad, Hay House, 2005.

up this practice throughout the year, then believe it or not, you will be a different person in 12 months!

The Heart-Brain Relationship

Have you ever considered that from the standpoint of human anatomy, there are more lines of communication from the heart to the brain than there are from the brain to the heart? I believe that the body's need for the brain to hear from the heart is symbolic. Many of today's leaders derive their training style from books, lectures, and working seminars, which present their material as simply a collection of facts, graphs, and catchy phrases that one can learn and store in their brain for future use. While these facts may be practicable, even necessary, presenting facts without emotion limits their usefulness for humble leaders. For example, how often have you experienced knowing that you should consider yourself personally responsible for xyz, but because you don't feel this "in your bones" nothing changes? I strongly encourage you to consider how your heart determines not just your feelings but your perception, your priorities, and your actions. It is my opinion that it pays to listen to our hearts and the hearts of others. As I reflect on the behavior of many successful people it seems clear that what people truly care about dictates their actions. Taking a look at someone's planner or their checkbook reveals the priorities that they care the most about. I believe you will find that the answers to these questions tell you where one's heart lies. If our life decisions follow the leadings of our hearts, make sure the commitments we make to ourselves and others stem from head knowledge, and are rooted in the fertile soul of feeling that prioritize its development and growth.

Affirmations Generate Habits

I often say that humble leadership is a way of life. In a sense, one may say it is an expression of our habits relative to our relationship with others. Since much is called for if one is to achieve the many goals suggested or meet the standards of humble leadership set forth in this book, an argument for creating new habits is in order and methods as to "how-to" will be necessary. During the writing of this book I have interviewed a number of very successful people who hold responsible leadership positions. As you would expect, the why's and how's—why is this "good" leadership behavior important and how does one develop this "good" leadership behavior—always come up. Effective leaders are steeped in good habits, these habits are recognized and admired, and their importance is assumed; however, how they come about remains a mystery for many. How does one make well-accepted principles and values move from head-knowledge to heart-knowledge, become a part of life, and begin to be practiced subconsciously—without thought—from habit?

Habits, good or bad, come from repeated behaviors and are imprinted in our neural pathways. These habits often go unnoticed in those exhibiting them, because a person does not often engage in self-analysis when undertaking routine tasks. As this repetition gives rise to consistent behavior, it begins to form the person you are, the things you believe, and the personality you present to others. Did you ever say to yourself, "Why did I do that?" Habit! Thus, if the principles of leadership are not imprinted in one's neural pathways and have not become habits, it is unlikely that they will be applied routinely. Assuming this to be the case, new behaviors must be developed, they must become automatic, and this, of course, is habit formation.

It is well established that old habits are hard to break, and new habits are hard to form. However, it is possible to form new habits through repetition and these new habits can replace old ones we wish to break. As we have learned from personal experience, when behaviors are repeated in a consistent environment, there is an incremental increase in the link between the environment and the action. Assuming this behavior is repeated in the "leadership environment," it increases the automatic nature of the behavior in that environment.

To form a new habit, we identify the behavior we want to employ, turn to our power of visualization (we imagine ourselves performing the desired behavior) and exercise our power of discipline in support of new habit formation. Once we "see" the desired performance, we must exercise the determination to commit that performance to memory and apply it until its application becomes second nature!

Perception plays a critical role in the area of visualization and understanding it can significantly improve both the quality and the quantity of information made available to us. Perception is the organization, identification and interpretation of that which we see, hear, smell, or touch, and the brain's perceptual systems actively and pre-consciously attempt to make sense of their input. The senses enable us to understand the presented information of that which is around us. Perception is also shaped by our learning, memory, and expectation.

Earlier in this chapter, we considered the power we have over our own DNA, but did you know our perception of our environment can activate certain genes? According to H. F. Nijhout when a gene product is needed, a signal from its environment activates expression of that gene.[104] As suggested by Dr. Bruce H. Lipton in his book *Biology of Beliefs,* "Just like a single cell, the character of our lives is determined not by our genes but by our responses to the environmental signals…"[105] When it comes to genetic control, we must keep in mind that the environment plays a critical role. Our perception of the totality of circumstances surrounding us determines who we are because that perception, or those beliefs, control the genes that control life.

Visualization, for our purposes, is the development of the mental image or picture in our mind of an experience taking place when the event is not actually present in the senses. We see ourselves performing said action somewhere at some time in our environment. For example, if I would like to habitually recognize good behavior in someone else, I visualize myself expressing gratitude to others for a job well done or any other positive event and experience the reinforcing, emotional satisfaction for performing this act. Or, assuming I wanted to be a better listener, I may see myself in

---

104. Nijhout, H. F. "Problems And Paradigms: Metaphors and the Role of Genes in Development." *BioEssays*, vol. 12, no. 9, 1990, pp. 441–446.

105. Lipton, Bruce. *The Biology of Belief: Unleashing the Power of Consciousness, Matter and Miracles.* Carlsbad, Hay House, 2005.

a variety of situations where others are speaking and, while I am eager to make an input, I have decided to remain quiet, possibly take notes, and delay speaking until there is a lull in the conversation taking place. These and many other examples require some degree of discipline. If I have been a poor listener for many years, it is unlikely I will become a good listener overnight.

It was many years ago when I began as a sales representative for The Upjohn Company. After two field assignments as a "detail man" and one as a district manager, I was moved into the home office to be, among other things, a sales-oriented, scientific copywriter in our Sales Education Department. The results of my effort were "sales education copy" for the Sales Force and, on occasion, formed the basis for advertising copy. I had no writing experience, did not consider myself to be a creative person, and felt completely lost. Other than an occasional "You can do it," followed by a positive, "slap on the back," I got little encouragement. I began reading ads in journals where pharmaceuticals were being promoted. I paid attention to what I thought their message was, how their message compared with that of another (often a competitor), the font size of the copy and its impact, and color of the visuals and the impression they made on me. While I was not responsible for advertising copy nor layout, I visualized myself doing just that. I also began visualizing our sales representatives as "living" advertisements in the health professional's office. With that endpoint in mind, I exercised the discipline necessary to read as many ads as possible (I use the word "discipline" here because, after a few days of reading ads, they become about as interesting as reading the phone book!). Then I would remove those ads from the journal and attach them to the walls of my office. It wasn't very long before all walls were covered with ads, and I was reminded of my responsibility every time I walked through the door. This experience enabled me to see myself as a scientific copywriter whose effort would result in the use of the company's products.

There is a power within that can absolutely change your life and that power—visualization—is easy to unleash and harness. Visualization teaches your brain to come up with the resources you need, enhances motivation and sets you off in a positive direction. It does require discipline, however.

Do you remember the last time you read a book or left an event highly motivated—excited about making a change in your life? Your behavior? You were determined to be different. You said, "I mean it; I am going to become the person I just read about/heard about!" But after a few days, your motivation began to diminish. You experienced some change—de minimis at best—but not the kind that you so earnestly would like to have seen. Now, that is the kind of experience most of us have when attempting to change old habits or develop new ones. It is at this time when many of us give up. Don't do it! Simply make up your mind as to what you want to do, see yourself doing it, and enjoy the journey!

Remember, while we live in an "instant society," a society where it seems that everything comes at the push of a button, there is no such thing as an instant habit or behavior formation. Even though I would love to give you, my readers, the three easy steps to new behavior formation, it simply doesn't work that way. Some of us think that discipline in our daily lives has disappeared from our culture. However, it is the path we must follow if we are to develop the behavior(s) common to highly effective leaders. It is necessary that we set our goal—one (or more) that is *s*pecific, one that can be *m*easured, one that can be *a*chieved, one that is *r*ealistic and is *t*ime bound—these elements are commonly referred to as "SMART" goals. Once the goal(s) has been established, the focus must be directed regularly on achieving that goal.

James Clear, an author and photographer, who writes about behavioral psychology, habit formation, and performance improvement, studies successful people across a wide range of disciplines—entrepreneurs, artists, athletes, and more—to uncover the habits and routines that make these people the best at what they do. In his book *Atomic Habits: An Easy & Proven Way to Build Good Habits & Break Bad Ones*, he offers what he calls "The 3 R's of Habit Change: How To Start New Habits That Actually Stick."[106] The 3 R's are a reminder (the trigger that initiates the behavior);

---

106. Clear, James. *Atomic Habits: An Easy & Proven Way to Build Good Habits & Break Bad Ones*. Avery Publishing Group, 2018.

routine (the behavior itself... the action you take); and reward (the benefit you gain from doing the behavior.

As you study the subject of habit formation in more detail and come up with formulas that work for you, I suggest you include the value of affirmations. On a personal note, affirmations have worked exceptionally well for me over the years, and I continue to use them daily. As was the case in the vignette above, an affirmation was my first "R" (trigger). I wrote the affirmation in the present tense in order to program my brain to move me in the direction of my goal. When I posted the ads on my office wall, the affirmation I expressed was: "I am an effective, creative ad-writer." I chose a specific desired end result, described that end result in as few words as possible, wrote it down and, using post-it notes, set these reminders everywhere reasonable, e. g., on the bathroom mirror, inside notebooks, inside briefcases, on the dashboard of my automobile.

Today, if I become aware that I am falling short of exercising a behavior that would be useful in a relationship with others, I study the desired behavior, condense my findings to a few memorable words, then repeat those words, in a positive fashion, over and over to myself for an extended period of time. In a sentence, I know that I move toward my dominant thought(s) and am *affirming* that I am the person who exercises that desired behavior. I make sure that the "affirmation" is in keeping with all requirements of the SMART goal.

A great deal of study has focused on habit formation. While much has been learned in this area, remember that there is no "magic bullet." Rather than finding a single formula that works, we find that there are thousands. The "goal approach" works across the board, but some of us have not reached the required level of discipline. Individuals and habits are all different, and the specifics of finding the right formulae for creating a new habit in our lives differ from person to person and behavior to behavior. New habit formation isn't easy and can be very time-consuming. Let there be no question, though—making habits of the many principles of good leadership are worth the effort! Therefore, we must ask the question, do I want to be a good leader? Do I want to be a part of the growth and development of others? Do I really want to experience the joy that flows from others' experiencing the satisfaction of a job well done? Let's get to work!

The Role of Purpose

More than one-hundred and fifty years ago, Charles L. Dodgson, the author of *Alice In Wonderland* wrote: "If you don't know where you're going, any road will get you there."[107] It is impossible for me to think of this line without thinking of "purpose." Likewise, I can't think of "purpose" without thinking of these lines: "Why am I here?"; "What is my reason for being?"; "Why was I created?"; "Why do I go to work?".

A number of years ago Richard Duane (Rick) Warren, New York Times Best Selling Author and Senior Pastor of Saddleback Church in Lake Forest, California, wrote the book, *The Purpose Driven Life: What on Earth Am I Here for,* which was intended to be read as a daily inspiration.[108] As I became aware of the extent to which this book influenced lives of individuals from all walks of life, I began looking more carefully at the term, "purpose" and the influence it has on individuals and institutions. Therefore, my understanding of the word is that it describes the reason I do something. It clarifies my intentions, provides a motivation focus, energizes me toward accomplishing goals, helps me understand the "big picture," and identifies the small steps I must take to finish well. To be sure, all of the foregoing and more are necessary when my purpose is to support the flourishing of others.

Purpose answers the question, "Why?" Why do I get up in the morning? Why do I eat bread? Why do I love someone? Why do I go to work? It seems there is no end to the number of "why" questions and in every answer, there is something said that relates to purpose.

---

107. Carroll, Lewis (Charles L. Dodgson). *Alice's Adventures In Wonderland.* London, Macmillan Nov. 26, 1865.

108. Warren, Rick. *The Purpose-Driven Life: What on Earth Am I Here for?* Zondervan, 2016.

What is the role of purpose in the business sector? Roy M. Spence is the chairman and co-founder of an Austin, Texas-based advertising agency, GSD&M.

The GSD&M website, "Our Story," describes a few University of Texas graduates who, in 1971, proved to all interested parties they could open what ended up being a national advertising agency in a little Texas town we know as Austin. These courageous young people, full of ideas and a commitment to making their contribution, helped elect a president, launch Southwest Airlines, and contribute to Walmart's becoming the largest retailer in the world! As the years passed and their bravery continue to grow, they became known for their role in helping many brands we know today. Their mode of behavior begins with honesty and a serious interest in the success of their clients.

GSD&M's purpose is to "Do whatever it takes to grow our clients' business so that they can fulfill their purpose." A book authored by Spence and Haley Rushing titled: *It's Not What You Sell, It's What You Stand For*, was intended to be a textbook or manual for the brand management model pioneered by GSD&M called "Purposed-Based Branding." As stated by Spence:

> In a company without purpose, people have no idea what they're really there to do. They often look to the competition to decide what to do rather than navigate by their own sense of what's right. With a purpose in place, an organization knows its reason for being and is driven to perform and innovate. Purpose sets you apart from the competition, authenticates your brand, inspires passion in your people and helps you achieve the impossible.[109]

I have watched and listened to Roy Spence numerous times via YouTube and have always been inspired to maintain a focus on "purpose." I urge you to develop a similar focus. As you continue to grow as a *humble leader*, your

---

109. Spence, Roy, and Haley Rushing. *It's Not What You Sell, It's What You Stand for: Why Every Extraordinary Business Is Driven by Purpose.* Portfolio/Penguin, 2011.

understanding of the need to answer the question, "why" will become of untold value!

Simon O. Sinek is a British/American author, motivational speaker, and marketing consultant who published the best-selling book, *Start With Why: How Great Leaders Inspire Everyone to Take Action.* I had the privilege of meeting Simon a few years ago and, along with a few others, spent an evening listening to him present and was eventually able to discuss with him his views on why the leader should start with "why" since he asserted that it inspires everyone to take action. In his opinion, there are two main ways to influence human behavior: manipulation and inspiration, and he argues that inspiration is the more powerful and sustainable of the two. He says that people are inspired by a sense of purpose (or "Why") and that this should come first, before How and What.[110]

I saw the truth of this firsthand when I had the privilege of joining Dean Mark Reynolds and his leadership team as a consultant at the University of Maryland's Dental School. Early on we were engaged in discussions related to leadership development, which uncovered the need to develop a strategic plan that would guide the school during the coming years. The first step of this process was to establish a "purpose statement." We needed to answer the question: "Why do we come to work each day?" After numerous hours of discussion over a period of weeks, it was decided that the purpose was to advance oral health because good oral health is integral to the total health of all persons. That purpose, now stated on the school's website as, "Advancing Oral Health, Improving Lives" marked the beginning of the entire plan. And, while it takes strategic plans time to be fully accepted by many institutions, this school fully intended to implement the plan, driven by their newly defined purpose.

Purpose moves people to make things happen. Purpose inspires us to stay true to ourselves and the institutions we serve. Purpose encourages us to work hard, remain focused and "keep the faith," even when nobody else

---

110. Sinek, Simon. *Start with Why: How Great Leaders Inspire Everyone to Take Action.* Penguin Business, 2019.

believes. As Colin Powell said a few years ago, "A dream doesn't come true through magic; it takes sweat, determination, and hard work."[111] Some who read my championing of purpose here will not find themselves swayed, but my conviction is sound and based on many years of experience. When I begin coaching a new client and I emphasize the need for a purpose, the immediate pushback is: "I don't have a purpose and have never given it any thought." Furthermore, the person finds difficulty coming up with a purpose because they believe they have little evidence of their own value and the multitude of contributions he or she can make throughout the years ahead. To be sure, however, it always proves worth the effort to go through the laborious process of establishing an answer to the "why" question for your being. If an individual's self-esteem falls short of the ideal, it is often due to the fact that it is entwined with a fear of vulnerability. This fear of vulnerability encourages our self-centered tendencies, because instead of musing on how we could improve the lives of others, we are focusing on hiding our weaknesses and insecurities. Considering the question of our purpose and our true value frees us to appreciate the value of others and how we may serve the world. It took me a while to think through and answer that same question for myself but as you will see later my purpose is set clearly before me. Therefore, I know my personal responsibility, and the challenges that must be faced while attempting to benefit others by the way I live. I know myself and the pursuit of my purpose is worthier than my own fulfillment, peace of mind, happiness, ambition and career.

Humble leaders have a purpose in all that they do! I challenge you to find your purpose!

Achieving Personal Mastery

Personal mastery is critical to success in any endeavor. It is the end result of both knowing why we are placed on this earth and taking full, personal responsibility for deciding what we will do with our time, talents, and treasure. One's purpose will become clear when they carefully evaluate

---

111. Powell, Colin. Pass It On: Inspirational Quotes. https://www.passiton.com/inspirational-quotes/7750-a-dream-doesnt-become-reality-through-magic-it.

what they do throughout the course of each day, study their strengths and weaknesses, and decide how much they will give of themselves to achieve mastery.

As I wrote the above paragraph, Linda Ellis' poem "The Dash" came most vividly to my mind. This poem was delivered at a man's funeral and referenced the deceased's year of birth and the year of his death. However, as the title of the poem indicates, the man's life that took place between those dates were what mattered most, what took place during that dash.

During coaching sessions, I often ask my client, "What is the legacy you would like to leave when you depart this earth?" In most cases, the person says, "I am so busy trying to keep up with the requirements of the life I am living. I haven't given a 'legacy' much thought." For the rare individual who has given thought to how they want to be remembered, I ask, "Do you have a well-defined purpose that will guide you to that end?"

The point is that we all begin life with the potential to become who we want to be; we only need to seize it! Furthermore, it is our duty to leave inspiration for others to do the same. Maintain a constant awareness of how you live each day. Ask the question, "Am I better today than I was yesterday? And not as good as I will be tomorrow?" Without belaboring the point, once you get a picture of what kind of legacy you want to leave, form a clear purpose to guide you, so you will be able to end well.

On a personal note, I have a pretty good idea as to how I want to be remembered, and my own purpose statement reads as follows:

I shall take every opportunity each day to develop and share my God-given talents and abilities to further the flourishing of humankind.

It took a number of years to come to this understanding of my purpose, and it was something I did have to come to understand; it is not just a mere formulation of niceties. This purpose has simplified and directed the planning of my days, and while there continues to be bumps along the way, I can always end the day with, "I lived my dash and did my best."

APPLICATION QUESTIONS

- Do you feel there is value in a scientific explanation of certain behaviors? Why? If you did not have a scientific background, what would be your approach to using laboratory findings to make your point?

- Do you agree with the above argument supporting the value of listening to one's heart when engaged in leading an organization? Why?

- What is the primary role of "habits" in the humble leadership process? Do you agree with the importance of affirmations? Why?

- What are your views on the importance of purpose in one's personal and professional life?

- Explain how you would discuss the importance of personal mastery with one of your followers. How would you help them establish measurements for progress?

- Time Magazine carried a series of articles that asked the question, "What's wrong with the world?" G. K. Chesterton, a British journalist, novelist, essayist, and poet, wrote the editor saying, "It is me!" Where do you stand on this question?

- As of today, 27 April 2020, we are continuing our walk through the paths of the coronavirus pandemic. As you have witnessed the leadership in our country and that around the world and assessed the quality of leadership, what is your opinion?

Recommended Further Reading

The following titles may provide insightful information to the formation of habits.

1. *Atomic Habits: An Easy & Proven Way to Build Good Habits & Break Bad Ones* by James Clear

2. *The Power of Habit: Why We Do What We Do in Life and Business* by Charles Duhigg

3. *Mindset: The New Psychology of Success* by Carol Dweck

4. *Habit Stacking: 127 Small Changes to Improve Your Health, Wealth, and Happiness* by Steve Scott

5. *The Art of Good Habits: Health, Love, Presence, and Prosperity* by Nathalie Herrman

6. *Willpower: Rediscovering the Greatest Human Strength* by Roy F. Baumeister and John Tierney

7. *The ONE Thing: The Surprisingly Simple Truth Behind Extraordinary Results* by Gary Keller

8. *High Performance Habits: How Extraordinary People Become That Way* by Brendon Burchard

9. *Making Good Habits, Breaking Bad Habits: 14 New Behaviors That Will Energize Your Life* by Joyce Meyer

10. *The Now Habit: A Strategic Program for Overcoming Procrastination and Enjoying Guilt-Free Play* by Neil Fiore, Ph.D

In Conclusion

The life of a humble leader is difficult. This is a truism, and all you have read up to now is strong supporting evidence of this fact. The fully present person, one where the totality of their thoughts and actions are focused on the individuals and matters at hand, is rarely if ever seen. Nevertheless, your followers depend on you to effectively exercise the level of ability you have developed to successfully transform a bad situation into something good and a good situation into something better! You will recall, when leaving your high school, college, or institution of even higher learning, there was at least one teacher or professor who said, "You must be a life-long learner!" Truer words were never spoken when considering your quest to be a humble leader. You must be able to apply your personal agency and total capability to originate and direct actions to influence the flourishing of the human condition. I have argued that humble leadership is the most effective way to change cultures and catapult institutions to higher levels of performance. Furthermore, I have argued that humble leadership uniquely equips us to contribute to the flourishing of others. I wholeheartedly encourage you to challenge my position and continue your own research! The fact that you selected this book and made it this far tells me that there is a core you who knows they have a responsibility to share their value with others and become better equipped to do just that.

As I bring this book to a close, I remind you that to lead others, you must lead yourself first. To lead yourself, you must know who you are and why you are here. With this in mind, I leave you with these final questions:

- What is my identity? Do I have a sense of self that is durable, a sense of self-worth?

- Do I have the conviction and flaming passion to continuously develop my talents and contribute to the flourishing of others?

- Character demands that we lead in the effort to make the world and all its institutions a better place in which to live and work, and, when we face troubles that are sure to come, our leadership spirit is rekindled?

- When you come to the end of your professional career, what legacy would you like to leave by which we may remember you?

Appendix I

This eulogy offers more information on an individual who embodied the elements of humble leadership as described throughout this book. This man influenced the pattern of behavior that I would develop and apply for more than thirty years. While these words fall short of describing the real Malcolm G. Rogers, they and my memories of him and our many experiences shape a medium that continues to fuel the application of my purpose today.

Presented
To
Malcolm Rogers' Celebrants of His Life
The First Presbyterian Church
Florence, South Carolina

A few weeks ago, I completed 80 years of life. As I look at the many gray hairs scattered throughout this congregation, that fact is not unique to me. I mention it, however, largely because of the man represented before us in this casket, played a large role in my dressing in an acceptable fashion, seeing many of the major cities throughout the United States and around the world, eating in some of the world's greatest restaurants, enjoying the finest of wines, and making many everlasting friends.

The title I have given these comments is: Malcolm G. Rogers, the Modern-day Barnabas—God's Man of Encouragement and Inspiration.

Those of us in the world of business tend to affix ourselves to an unstable foundation that is continually shifting. As Peter Seaver reminded me yesterday, however, the man we honor today never moved, never left us standing alone; he was our anchor for the storms of our business life. He was always encouraging… always an inspiration… the consummate winner!

As I look around this sanctuary, I see enough white hair to state with some accuracy that many of us have been to more than one gathering like this. There have been times when I felt, possibly like you, that a highly skilled speech writer put words to paper that someone else delivered to the congregation—the words did not necessarily reflect who we knew that person to be. Such is not the case this afternoon. I put these words on this paper and to the best of my ability I will reflect, in a very small way, one of the finest, most respected persons to walk the face of this earth.

Those of you who witnessed in person or by television the praise afforded our late president George Herbert Walker Bush you will remember words suggesting that politicians should follow the "delicious" example of President Bush and learn from his life story. You may also remember the statement, and I quote, "He was a man of such great humility." The speaker added that those who travel the high road of humility in Washington, DC, are not bothered by heavy traffic. These were the words of Alan Simpson, the American politician who represented Wyoming in the United States Senate until his retirement in 1997. These words also apply to Malcolm Rogers.

If you knew Malcolm Rogers as many in this congregation and I did, you will know the value of following the "delicious" example of this man and learning from his life story. Also, if you knew Malcolm, you know there were times when he had a short fuse. His ability to express his displeasure with emotion and clarity, especially when his people were mistreated, was unequaled… I tried to disappear at those times.

On Wednesday morning of last week, I read a daily devotion published by the Ravi Zacharias International Ministries. Written by Nathan Betts, a portion of it goes like this: "The first Christmas after my father passed away, I remember sitting in my parents' home on Christmas Eve, wanting to have some time alone to think about my dad. Being the father of a young family myself, it had a been a day full of frantic activity getting ready for Christmas. Christmas music was playing, sweet and savory aromas of cooking and baking were wafting from the kitchen, and our children were chasing each other throughout the house. So many signs of life surrounded me. Yet, I could not shake the reality of a profound absence. My father was not there."[112]

Betts wrote that he decided to go for a walk on that cold, December afternoon, reminisce about the good ole days, and pretend his dad was walking with him. As he reflected on those earlier times, he thought of how happy Dad would be were he with his son during that stroll down memory lane.

Mr. Betts continued, and I quote again, "I realize this might sound strange, but this was part of processing my father's loss. I walked and talked to my dad for another twenty minutes before heading home. Minutes before I walked onto my parents' street, I decided to be quiet. There was not a sound in the air, except for my footsteps. Yet, what I heard shocked me. As each one of my steps touched the icy ground, my footsteps sounded strangely like my father's footsteps. In the pace and frequency of each footfall I could actually hear the sound of my father walking. Without knowing it, my pace of walking reflected the way my father walked. In hearing my footsteps, I was again reminded of my father's absence."[113]

While the devotion comes to an end with an emphasis on Christ, Christmas, and the untold value of knowing God is with us, the influence of dad in our lives is immense and never ends.

---

112. Betts, Nathan. "Garden in the Snow." https://www.rzim.org/read/a-slice-of-infinity/garden-in-the-snow.

113. ibid.

Malcolm Rogers was not my dad. I do not walk like Malcolm Rogers and never will. I did not fill the shoes of Malcolm Rogers, and never will. But my story doesn't end here.

At this point, Dr. Charles Stanley would pause and say, "Are you listening? If so, say 'Amen.' I have four or five more brief points I want to make, and they are important."

Number 1. Just over 56 years ago, Billie and I sat in a hotel room in Charlotte, North Carolina, for our final interview for a job with The Upjohn Company, one of our nation's premier pharmaceutical companies at the time. Shortly after returning to our home in Greenville, SC, we were offered the job, which turned out to be one of the greatest experiences of a lifetime. What I learned over the following years is that Malcolm saw in me value that I had not seem in myself. The message to me was to look for the best in all people. When you do, you will find it!

Number 2. Just over 51 years ago, I sat in Malcolm's office in Miami, Florida. He was sales manager at that time and had convinced "home office" that I was qualified to be one of his district managers. As I sat on his sofa in front of his big desk with him on the other side, he cleaned the center portion of the desk, placed his hands about 24 inches apart, looked me in the eye and said, "Harold, I want you to use your imagination for just a minute. Between my hands is a curled stack of rope and is as long as you imagine it to be." He then pretended to slide the imagined rope across the desk toward me, then said, "Take all the rope you want, take it as far as you would like, and become the leader you are destined to be. There will be bumps along the way… there will be times when you will fall… when that happens, remember, I'm here to catch you."

I learned from point Number 2 the value of knowing and respecting your fellow men, having compassion for others, and having the courage to take a personal risk on those who have yet to walk your path.

Number 3. Malcolm told me more than once, "Do not embarrass the boss and dress well." I tried not to embarrass the boss and from him, I learned how to dress and while my wardrobe will never match his, I never cease trying.

Number 4. He taught me the correct behavior common to those in the C-Suite. I learned from those instructions and he made sure I had a seat at the C-Suite tables.

Number 5, my last and most important lesson. While visiting with him at the retirement home and after he had given me the honor of speaking to you today, I asked Malcolm if he was confident in his relationship with Christ. His answer was an emphatic yes. Since his answer was so immediate and with emphasis, I asked if he would tell me more. He said that when they were living in Kalamazoo, the Billy Graham team had come to the Notre Dame football stadium, which is on the school's campus, just North of South Bend, Indiana. The evening's event was coming to an end, and a few thousand attendees were singing, "Just As I Am." As I remember his story, Susan, you said to him and your mom, "Let's go down." The three of you did!

From that, I was reminded of the importance and value of keeping Christ first in my life.

Malcolm Rogers took full responsibility for his life and the impact it had on others.

Malcolm was gifted, equipped, and enabled to fulfill God's purpose in his life. He did just that.

Billie and I loved him and his dear wife, Elma, without condition and respected them beyond measure. Our prayer is that our memory of him remains and continues to guide each of us until the day we meet him in the presence of our Lord, Jesus Christ, face to face.

Amen.

Appendix II

In this section you will find information on three individual assessments: the Big Five Aspects Scale, Gallup's CliftonStrengths, and an example of the 360 Assessment in full. Additionally included is the author's report of the Small Group Initiative for the University of Maryland, School of Dentistry to serve as an example of a successful use of small groups within an institution. In the report, readers will find tips for designing their own program, selecting participants, establishing a meeting schedule, formulating the meeting agenda, and so forth.

Any assessment found in this section is available to all who read this book. Please feel free to use these assessment in your own leadership position. They can also be found at this website: https://www.internasource.com/.

The Big Five Aspects Scale

It is my view that to lead others, one must lead him or herself first. To lead oneself, one must know oneself! At this point in my professional career, I tend to favor the "Big Five Aspects Scale" mentioned earlier. I have completed this assessment, and the results have proven to be very useful. The Big Five Aspects provide information regarding *openness, conscientiousness, extroversion, agreeableness,* and *neuroticism.* Here I present an introduction to each of these traits, and I encourage you to find the Big Five Aspects assessment online and take it yourself!

Openness

Openness is the primary dimension of creativity, artistic interest, and intelligence, particularly verbal intelligence, in the Big Five personality trait scientific model. The open person endorses new adventures and unusual ideas and demonstrates imagination, intellectual curiosity, and an appreciation for a variety of personal experiences, as well as the experiences of others. This openness to experience is a measure of interest in novelty, literature, abstract thinking, philosophy, a willingness to try new things, as well as sensitivity to aesthetic emotions and beauty. Your openness enlivens your awareness of and respect for others' feelings who may hold unconventional beliefs. Openness encourages strong support of equal opportunity, personal freedom, the right to choose, the right to diversity, the right of one to love whom one loves in the way that one may desire.

It is important to develop and demonstrate an appropriate level of this dimension since it means you are open to all possible perspectives, even to those you disagree with. If you consider your openness suboptimal, search the literature or seek council. While openness is considered an innate quality, it can be improved.

Conscientiousness

Conscientious people are extremely dutiful. They work remarkably hard and hate wasting time. They keep promises to do something regardless of circumstances and without finding excuses. They are extraordinarily decisive, neat, organized, future-oriented, and reliable, and not easily distracted. The conscientious person is aware, anticipating approaching danger to self or others. She or he is attentive and cares for the well-being of others whether they be individuals or members of the community. This person tends to show self-discipline and aims for achievement against all measures or outside expectations.

How do you measure up? As is the situation with openness, it can be improved if necessary.

Extroversion

Extroversion is the primary element of positive emotion and a measurement of general sensitivity to positive emotions such as hope, joy, anticipation and approach, particularly in social situations. This dimension describes the tendency to seek activity and to enjoy the company of other people. The extrovert is characterized by breadth of activities (as opposed to depth), and/or a pronounced engagement with the external world.

This dimension deserves a personal story since some of you may feel that extraversion, an important quality, is not nor will be one of your "long suits."

As a somewhat shy, reserved person during my early years, I was comfortable with the idea of spending my "professional life" in a science laboratory. This idea was confirmed as I entered college and completed all the scientific requirements to become a pharmacist. After a few short years practicing that profession in the community and hospital settings, it became quite clear that neither venue was going to satisfy my career desires, even though I didn't actually know what my desires were at the time. While searching for the "right" opportunity, I had become professional friends with Byron O'dell, a sales representative with The Upjohn Company. Byron was not shy, but he was reserved; not an extrovert, but sufficiently social. After extensive conversations, he convinced me, the "non-extrovert," that I could surely be a salesman if he could, and in my opinion, he was quite good. Based on those conversations, I joined Upjohn.

Fortunately, I enjoyed only limited success early and learned almost immediately that my style would not serve me well over time. I concluded that if I intended to have an impact on healthcare I would have to move up in the company. To move up, my shy, reserved approach would be limiting. Something had to change, and that change meant breaking out of my shell.

Forcing myself to give up the comfort of a shy, reserved lifestyle, I participated in the Dale Carnegie Sales Course, followed immediately by approximately three years in the Toastmasters International Club of Orlando,

Florida. While I will never be the world's notable extrovert, I now rank in the 88th percentile according to the "Big Five" assessment, and these two early experiences paved the way for change and a successful career.

There is much more to be said about extroversion than I have said here and these few words do not begin to establish the value of this attribute. I encourage you to become exceedingly aware of the literature and develop this quality to its fullest possible extent. It will surely serve you and others well.

Agreeableness

There is a direct relationship between agreeableness and interpersonal interactions. The agreeable person tends to be compassionate rather than antagonistic or indifferent toward others. This person is nice, polite, considerate, generous, trusting and trustworthy, compliant and kind, to mention a few qualities. They also have a general concern for social harmony and value getting along with others. He or she is helpful and willing to compromise their interests.

Agreeableness is a complex and desirable trait. In addition to demonstrating a high level of agreeableness, the humble leader will study this element very carefully since it has such a positive impact on followers.

Neuroticism (Emotional Instability)

The person ranking high on this scale tends to experience negative emotions, such as anger, anxiety or depression, and a low tolerance for stress or aversive stimuli. A high ranking on this scale also refers to one's degree of emotional stability. This is important in that humble leaders usually exhibit a stable and calm personality.

Gallup's CliftonStrengths

Gallup's CliftonStrengths guides the individual in the identification of their top five of thirty-four major strengths, which allows one to keep in check strengths, which used to excess become weaknesses, better enabling them to establish positive relationships. Here is a description directly from their website, and I encourage you to check it out: "The CliftonStrengths Assessment Unlocks Your Talent DNA... CliftonStrengths helps you aim your purpose at greater performance... CliftonStrengths helps you harness what makes you uniquely powerful."[114]

The 360 Assessment

The 360 Assessment design I use is based on the qualities discussed in Section II of the book. When I coach an individual and we decide to perform a 360 Assessment, the first step is for the individual to make a selection of the values, virtues, and behaviors discussed in this book on which they would like to be evaluated. Next, the person to be assessed selects six to eight individuals who know the person well and agrees to the relatively extensive, one-on-one interview. Prior to the interview, I send the below document to the interviewees so they have time to consider my questions in advance. The interviews are strictly confidential and when possible, face-to-face. The selection of individuals attempts to capture insight from all levels of the "workforce hierarchy": two or three subordinates, two or three equals, and two or three superiors. Each quality in the assessment is rated on a scale of one to five (five being the best rating) and all verbatims are recorded. When all interviews are completed, the findings are consolidated into a final report. I encourage you to review the material in this book, select the parameters of your own assessment, and ask a trusted and honest colleague or friend to conduct interviews of your six to eight individuals in

---

114. Gallup. "CliftonStrengths." May 2, 2020. https://www.gallup.com/cliftonstrengths/en/253850/cliftonstrengths-for-individuals.aspx?utm_source=google&utm_medium=cpc&utm_campaign=Strengths_ECommerce_Brand_Search_US&utm_content=%2Bstrengthsfinder%20%2Bassessment&gclid=Cj0KCQjwtLT1BRD9ARIsAMH3BtVHAfHEhO8TRoLSWYmaKiUNLn-8OH68FqsL2XL8nrwHOStuvlolCqAaApcsEALw_wcB.

your own circle. If you have any questions about this process, please do not hesitate to reach out to me by email (halchappelear@gmail.com).

Following is the 360 Assessment I use:

HUMBLE LEADERSHIP
A 360 ASSESSMENT
OF
COACHED PROFESSIONAL
2018

Following is a list of traits, qualities and competencies that describe inspiring, transforming leaders who derive personal and professional success via a focus on service to others. Following each major heading is a series of statements intended to "define" that trait, quality or competency.

After carefully reading each trait, quality or competency and considering the above person in light of your knowledge and understanding, please provide a rating (1 = lowest—5 = highest)

Character   Rating =

1. Relatively permanent traits

   a. Openness to experience—Appreciates art, emotions, adventure, unusual ideas… demonstrates imagination, curiosity… appreciates a variety of experiences, is intellectually curious… is sensitive to beauty and willing to try new things… creative and aware of their feelings, likely to hold unconventional beliefs.

   b. Conscientiousness—Tends to show self-discipline, act dutifully, and aim for achievement against measures or outside expectations.

c. Extroversion—Characterized by breadth of activities (as opposed to depth), pronounced engagement with the external world.

d. Agreeableness—Reflects individual differences in general concern for social harmony… value getting along with others… considerate, kind, generous, trusting, and trustworthy… helpful and willing to compromise their interests with others.

e. Neuroticism (Emotional Stability)—Tend to experience negative emotions, such as anger, anxiety, or depression… low tolerance for stress or aversive stimuli.

1. Stable moral qualities

    a. Virtues (habits of mind, heart, and behavior… developed through deliberate practice… moral excellence… existence or lack of)

    b. Humility—the foundation of all virtues… the whole moral life… necessary for the acquisition of the other virtues…

    c. Temperance—moderation or the ability to control one's self…

    d. Courage—acting correctly in the face of popular opposition, shame, scandal, discouragement or personal loss…

    e. Honesty—integrity, truthfulness, straightforwardness, trustworthiness, loyalty, fairness, sincerity…

5. Wisdom—what one does with what one knows... a habit of performing an action with the highest degree of acceptability under any given circumstance... avoid wrongdoing...

6. Faith—engendering confidence or trust... belief not based on proof...

7. Hope—the desire of something and expectation of receipt...

8. Love—the most excellent of all the virtues... human kindness,compassion... affection...

Interviewee Comments:

Communications   Rating =

1. Communicates well both verbally and in writing

2. Creates accurate and punctual reports

3. Delivers presentations

4. Shares information and ideas with others

5. Communicates in an open, authentic manner

6. Listens to others with understanding

7. Encourages feedback

8. Fosters a non-punitive atmosphere in which people can be frank and candid

9. Communicates decisions to others

Interviewee Comments:

Compassion   Rating =

1. Very caring, understanding, and forgiving

2. Has a deep awareness of the physical and/or mental pain of others, which is coupled with the wish to help alleviate this pain

3. Very sympathetic, tolerant, encourages friendships, promotes happiness and exhibits a loving demeanor

4. Effectively helps people focus on a common purpose

5. Promotes collaboration to find optimal win-win solutions to resolve conflict

6. Is concerned with the inner, deeper interests and well-being of team members

7. Considers the needs, feelings and concerns of others

8. Knows superiors, "equals," and subordinates well

Interviewee Comments:

Responsibility   Rating =

1. He/she maintains a focus on the philosophy of individual responsibility… takes full for what he/she does and the impact it has on others.

Hope   Rating =

1. Optimistic and provides hope for the future—something with expectation of its fulfillment

2. Provides direction, encourages faith and offers guidance

3. Makes one enthusiastic about tomorrow and good things to come

Interviewee Comments:

Managing Conflict   Rating =

1. Listens well, diffuses conflict before it starts

2. Finds causes of and solutions to problems, handles difficult people

Interviewee Comments:

Negotiation Skills   Rating =

1. Conducts positive negotiations

2. Able to compromise

3. Handles conflict, seeks common ground

4. Articulates own and other's goals

5. Stays focused on positive outcome

Interviewee Comments:

People Development   Rating =

1. Consistently treats people with dignity

2. Asks people what they need to do their work better; ensures that people receive the training they need to succeed

3. Provides effective coaching and developmental feedback in a timely manner

4. Provides effective recognition for others' achievements; rewards hard work and risk taking

5. Takes mentoring role

6. Challenges and develops employees

7. Accepts mistakes

8. Provides visibility/opportunity

Interviewee Comments:

Stability   Rating =

1. Is steadfast

2. Provides a solid foundation and exhibits constancy of character or purpose

3. Provides security, strength, support, and peace

4. Core values are stable

5. Can always be counted on in time of need.

6. Consistently acts with a high degree of integrity

Interviewee Comments:

Trust   Rating =

1. Deserves trust and confidence

2. Is dependable

3. Worthy of reliance

4. Faithful—steadfast in allegiance; honest—not deceptive or disposed to cheat or defraud

5. Responsible—worthy of being held accountable

6. Principled—high standards of rightness or morality

7. Ethical—conforms to accepted standards of social or professional behavior

8. Steadfast—unwavering or determined in purpose, loyalty, etc.

Interviewee Comments:

Building Partnerships   Rating =

1. Treats coworkers as partners, not competitors

2. Unites her organization into an effective team

3. Builds effective partnerships cross the institution

4. Discourages destructive comments about other people or groups

5. Builds effective alliances with other organizations

6. Creates a network of relationships that help to get things done

Interviewee Comments:

Creating a Shared Vision   Rating =

1. Creates and communicates a clear vision for the organization

2. Effectively involves people in decision-making

3. Inspires people to commit to achieving the vision

4. Develops an effective strategy to achieve the vision

5. Clearly identifies priorities

6. Seeks to stretch in setting strategic personal and organizational goals

Interviewee Comments:

Empowers People   Rating =

1. Builds people's confidence

2. Takes risks in letting others make decisions

3. Gives people the freedom they need to do their job well

4. Trusts people enough to let go (avoids micromanagement)

5. Effectively helps people focus on a common purpose

6. Considers the needs, feelings, and concerns of others

7. Places a high priority on coaching people as part of his/her job

Interviewee Comments:

Adaptability/Flexibility   Rating =

1. Adapts to change

2. Is open to new ideas

3. Takes on new responsibilities, handles pressure, and adjusts plans to meet changing needs

Interviewee Comments:

Creativity/Innovation   Rating =

1. Generates new ideas

2. Challenges the status quo

3. Takes risks, supports change, encourages innovation

4. Solves problems creatively

Interviewee Comments:

Internal Customer Focus   Rating =

1. Builds customer confidence

2. Is committed to increasing customer satisfaction

3. Sets achievable customer expectations

4. Assumes responsibility for solving customer problems

5. Ensures commitments to customers are met

6. Solicits opinions and ideas from customers

7. Responds to internal customers

Interviewee Comments:

Decision-making/Judgment   Rating =

1. Recognizes problems and responds

2. Systematically gathers information, sorts through complex issues, seeks input from others

3. Addresses root cause of issues, makes difficult decisions timely

4. Uses consensus when possible

5. Communicates decisions to others

6. Is proactive when the situation demands action

7. Pursues what he/she believes the right way versus what others want and need

Interviewee Comments:

Integrity/Ethics   Rating =

1. Deals with others in a straightforward and honest manner

2. Is accountable for actions

3. Maintains confidentiality

4. Supports institutions values

5. Conveys good news and bad

Interviewee Comments:

Interpersonal Skills   Rating =

1. Has good listening skills

2. Builds strong relationships

3. Is flexible/open-minded

4. Negotiates effectively

5. Solicits performance feedback and handles constructive criticism

6. Seeks collaborative decisions and conveys respect to those who disagree

Interviewee Comments:

Listening Skills   Rating =

1. Listens attentively to others (maintains eye contact, exhibits favorable body language)

2. Asks clarifying questions

3. Stays open to other viewpoints

4. Manages distractions and interruptions

5. Seeks understanding

Interviewee Comments:

Strategic Thinking   Rating =

1. Creates and communicates a long-term vision

2. Balances short- and long-term goals

3. Keeps own and team's work aligned with overall goals

4. Understands the market and can predict change

5. Understands the industry and the competition

6. Creates and adjusts strategic plans

Interviewee Comments:

Values   Rating =

1. Has and lives by a set of value that represents him/her at home and at work

2. Shows appreciation—takes a brief moment to say, "thank you"

3. Has a belief in others—an attitude/resolve to lift someone up when they are down

4. Is caring—caring for others as well as self-care

5. Shows commitment—shows loyalty… fulfilling a promise made

6. Shows compassion—takes care of self and others

7. Shown cooperation—focuses on the solution with others; courtesy; etc.

Interviewee Comments:

Problem solving   Rating =

1. Has a system for identifying, analyzing, and solving problems

2. Sees the "big" picture and avoids "crisis management"

3. Appreciates opinions that different from his/her own

Interviewee Comments:

Public Speaking   Rating =

1. Is the face of the institution, internally and externally

2. Able to clearly and confidently articulate institution's vision and the role it plays in the "bigger picture…"

Interviewee Comments:

Writing   Rating =

1. Has the ability to explain the logic of an idea in a succinct way

Interviewee Comments:

Diversity and Inclusion   Rating =

1. Embraces the value of diversity in people (including culture, race, sex, or age)

2. Effectively motivates people from different cultures or backgrounds

3. Recognizes the value of diverse views and opinions

4. Helps others appreciate the value of diversity

5. Actively expands her knowledge of other cultures (through interactions, language study, travel, etc.)

Interviewee Comments:

Technologically Savvy   Rating =

1. Strives to acquire the technological knowledge needed to succeed in tomorrow's world

2. Successfully recruits people with needed technological expertise

3. Effectively manages the issue of technology to increase productivity

Interviewee Comments:

Sharing Leadership   Rating =

1. Willingly shares leadership with the institution's partners

2. Defers to others when they have more expertise

3. Strives to arrive at an outcome *with* others (as opposed to *for* others)

4. Creates an environment where people focus on the larger good (avoids sub-optimization or "turfism")

5. Develops effective relationship with colleagues

6. Seeks collaborative decisions and conveys respect to those who disagree

Interviewee Comments:

Achieving Personal Mastery   Rating =

1. Deeply understands her own strengths and weaknesses

2. Invests in ongoing personal development

3. Stands up for what she believes in

4. Show composure when under pressure

5. Seeks to improve in response to constructive criticism

Interviewee Comments:

Humility (Score each as follows: 1—Almost never; 2—Occasionally; 3—Frequently)

 1. Is resistant to receiving help from others. ___

 2. Has unresolved conflicts with others. ___

 3. Is reluctant to tell others when wrong. ___

 4. Is offended when others correct. ___

 5. Is unwilling to yield to others, even with the most minor issues. ___

 6. Is upset when not recognized for personal achievements. ___

 7. Is jealous when peers are successful. ___

 8. Others consider him/her standoffish. ___

 9. Is self-conscious in public, overly concerned about what others think. ___

10. Remains stoic when overwhelmed by either sorrow or joy. __

11. Circle of friends is made up of very similar people—same color, same ethnicity, same socio-economic background. __

12. Has material possessions just to impress others. __

13. Doesn't particularly pay attention to the handicapped, the elderly, and small children. __

14. Has trouble remembering others' names. __

Interviewee Comments:

Leadership   Rating =

1. Engages in an inspiring, transforming relationship of influence

2. Interacts with others for the purpose of sharing a vision, values, and beliefs

3. Interaction style raises self and others to higher levels of morality, motivation, and achievement

4. Leads through change and adversity

5. Makes the tough call when needed

6. Builds consensus when appropriate

7. Motivates and encourages others

8. Places a high priority on coaching people as part of his/her job

9. Establishes clear performance expectations

10. Adapts his/her leadership style to the needs of individuals and situations

11. Provides specific direction when needed

12. Gives support and encouragement when needed

13. Delegates decisions and authority effectively

14. Creates an environment where people want to do their best for the organization

15. Ensures that people are properly trained and equipped to do excellent work

16. Is positive and upbeat

17. Encourages feedback

18. Gives criticism well

19. Trusted by others to maintain confidentiality

20. Consistently treats people with respect and dignity

21. Consistently acts with a high degree of integrity

22. Keeps his/her promises

23. Taking everything into account, how satisfied are you with him/her as a leader?

Interviewee Comments:

Management Skills

Since this is a book about leadership rather than management, I heartily recommend you become a serious student of that literature. One's commitment to good leadership requires a well-developed knowledge and understanding of the requirements for good management. As you know, there are many great resources in the marketplace. The writings of Peter Drucker mentioned earlier in this boot, got me off to a good start, a start that has developed into a terrific career.

ALL OF THE FOREGOING PROVIDES BACKGROUND FOR THE FOLLOWING QUESTIONS. PLEASE BE AS SPECIFIC AS POSSIBLE WITH YOUR ANSWERS.

1. What behaviors does the person currently demonstrate that contribute to his/her effectiveness as a leader?

2. Which behavior should he/she develop or enhance to be a more effective leader?

3. Which behavior should the person eliminate or reduce to be a more effective leader?

4. If he/she could change one thing about his/her leadership style, what would it be?

5. Additional Comments?

———————

Small Group Initiative for the University of Maryland, School of Dentistry

The Dean of the School of Dentistry at the University of Maryland expressed interest in improving employee engagement in his school. As a consultant to the Dean, I initiated a one-year trial program referred to as the Small Group Initiative. Following is the report of the trial provided the Dean in June 2019:

Employee Engagement Project
University of Maryland, Baltimore—School of Dentistry
2018-2019

This report is written in the first person. Unless stated otherwise, InternaSource LLC, IS, I, and Hal Chappelear are one and the same. It will present the "leadership role" assumed by IS to reach a successful end to the one-year trial period.

Situation Analysis

David Brooks wrote in his recent book, *The Second Mountain*, "For six decades the worship of the self has been the central occupation of our culture—molding the self, investing in the self, expressing the self. Capitalism, the meritocracy, and modern social science have normalized selfishness; they have made it seem that the only human motives that are real are the self-interested ones—the desire for money, status, and power." If one may assume that Brooks is somewhat correct in his assessment of our current society, it is no wonder that many of our Institution's top leaders are disturbed by a culture that represents this kind of behavior and are seriously concerned about its impact on employee engagement. There is no substitute for self-responsibility and respect for others.

The Gallup Organization has established, via extensive surveys and careful analyses, that less than one-third of the American Workforce is engaged in their jobs. This finding has remained true for several years. A "Climate Survey" (via Gallup) was completed throughout the UMB Campus during the Spring of 2016. During late-December 2017, Dean Mark Reynolds and I met with Dr. Roger Ward to discuss outcomes of the Survey. It was noted that the Survey was completed near the time of the "Baltimore Riots," which may have influenced the findings. It was also noted that the results suggested that employee engagement across all Schools were similar to the Gallup findings of the American Workforce.

To be sure, when employees are engaged, absenteeism is lower, turnover is lower, shrinkage (pilferage) is lower, employee safety incidents are lower, and patient safety incidents are lower. Additionally, all customer (patient) metrics are higher, productivity is higher, personal responsibility and respect for others is higher, as well as other relevant, institutional parameters.

Based on the foregoing, InternaSource LLC, with approval of Dean Reynolds, instituted the "Small Group Initiative" (SGI). Following extensive planning, the first of the Small Group Meetings took place on 25 June 2018. It was communicated to all interested in the project and participants that the purposes of the SGI was to improve employee engagement, thus improve psychosocial behavior of the workforce, and positively impact the culture of the institution.

This effort encourages more and closer relationships among employees. It also suggests the importance of a high score for each question or statement within the Gallup Survey since a high score implies the level of employee satisfaction and willingness to "go the extra mile." Following are the questions/statements:

0 How satisfied are you with your school as a place to work?

1. I know what is expected of me at work.

2. I have the materials and equipment to do my work right.

3. At work, I have the opportunity to do what I do best every day.

4. In the past seven days, I have received recognition or praise for doing good work.

5. My supervisor, or someone at work, seems to care about me as a person.

6. There is someone at work who encourages my development.

7. At work, my opinions seem to count.

8. The mission or purpose of my school makes me feel my job is important.

9. My fellow employees are committed to doing quality work.

10. I have a best friend at work.

11. In the last six months, someone has talked to me about my progress.

12. This last year, I have had opportunities at work to learn and grow.

As one reflects on possible responses to the above, one begins to realize the psychological and social (psychosocial) impact a high score has on the culture of an institution and why a focus on the psychosocial atmosphere is so important.

Program Design

Small Groups

Experience derived from religious, academic, and business institutions strongly suggests the value of small discussion groups when there is a need to enhance relationships and establish positive attitudes toward ideas—new and well-established—that are basic to advancement of the institution.

While small groups vary in size, we determined that 5 discussants and 1 facilitator would be appropriate. Our decision was based on the fact that the meeting would not exceed one hour, the agenda would include five topics, and it was desirable that each person be given time to express his or her thoughts on each topic. The latter derives from evidence that one's memory of the topic is enhanced when he or she actively participates in a discussion of that topic.

The Facilitator may participate in the discussion. However, his or her primary role includes the following: participate in two facilitator meetings each month to review discussions that took place during the previous month's small group meetings; develop agendas for each small group meeting; communicate the agenda to participating members before the meeting and assign a topic to each member; call the meeting to order and introduce the topics for discussion; keeping the meeting on schedule so that each participant has an opportunity to speak; end the meeting on time.

(Please note that Agendas will be described later.)

Selecting Participants

During a three-year period beginning in early, 2014, approximately 65 members of the School's Leadership, Faculty and Staff had participated in development programs implemented by InternaSource. The group was informed of the SGI, advised that its purpose was to improve employee engagement, and individuals were given the opportunity to volunteer to participate in a one-year trial period beginning 25 June 2018. From the group of volunteers, 48 were selected. This group was divided into 8 groups of 5 participants per group. The remaining 8 volunteers were designated "Facilitators." The Facilitators, as described above, were guided by InternaSource and were responsible for setting agendas, facilitating the meetings, and providing feedback.

Gallup Employee Engagement Survey

During the period July—August 2018, all group members were asked to complete the Engagement Survey. A total of 46 participants of the 48 selected completed the survey. As presented via the attached, 36% (approximately 17 individuals) were considered to be engaged in their jobs.

Meeting Schedule

Each Small Group Meeting takes place for a period of one hour on the fourth Monday of each month. Although there are occasional, slight variations in time and change in meeting days due to unavoidable conflicts, the schedule has been maintained.

The Facilitator's Meetings takes place on the first and third Monday of each month. This schedule is established so that on the first Monday, there is an opportunity to provide feedback pertaining to the previous fourth-Monday meeting and discuss opportunities for improvement. The third-Monday meeting is devoted to a review of previous meetings and development of an Agenda for the coming, fourth Monday **Small Group Meeting**.

Agenda

The agenda for the first meeting contained 6 topics (see attached). Item 1 on this agenda encouraged the group's getting to know each other and a document to facilitate this effort was provided. While some groups maintained this as an agenda item for a few of the following meetings, agendas were eventually reduced to 5 items as mentioned above. Following is a list of the topics and justification for their inclusion:

1. One of Gallup's Q^{12} questions

    The one-year trial period would permit discussion of each question, thus a greater understanding of that question and the possibility of improved behavior as one applied the behavior suggested by the question. High ratings on each of the Gallup questions mentioned above (Situation Analysis) relate to the benefits described.

2. Strategic Plan

    A most important aspect of implementing a plan is everyone's knowledge and understanding of the plan. With this in mind, a significant topic presented via the plan was included for discussion. A typical question to be answered was why is that item included in the plan and what will be the benefit when implemented?

3. Value

   The Campus and the Dental School have adopted 8 values regarded to be of major importance as the institution(s) comply with its (their) responsibilities as an employer and respected members of the community. While these values are visible in a variety of locations throughout the School and Campus, observable conduct doesn't always match that which is called for when that value is expected to reflect one's behavior.

   Including a "value" topic for discussion encourages a greater understanding of that value and a recognition of the importance of encouraging behavior in keeping with that value throughout the day's activities.

4. Miscellaneous

   This is a ten-minute segment where any individual may introduce a subject deemed important enough for group discussion

5. Action Plan

   At the end of the above discussions, an item of most importance was selected, and a plan of action is established to implement that item during the coming 4 weeks.

The above suggests a very orderly, precise approach to "covering a lot of ground in a short period of time." Such was not always the case for a variety of reasons. As the groups have become more focused, each one is coming closer to this paradigm.

Maintaining Interest

Projects, such as the Small Group Initiative, give rise to a fair amount of curiosity, commitment, and interest in the early stages. As time passes, however, other initiatives present and often provide a source of competition for one's attention. Aware that this Initiative was destined to be successful if maintained over an extended period, IS maintained constant (frequent) contact with individual members of the Small Groups with a focus on encouragement and an attempt to motivate each member to "stay the course." This effort, along with that of the Facilitators and the School's Leadership seems to be successful.

Findings

The primary purpose of this major, long-termed, labor-intensive effort was to impact, in a positive way, the culture of the Dental School and establish this institution as a "best place to work." It was determined that appropriate "job skills" characterized the School's work force. It was also determined that a focus on behavior, the psychosocial aspects of the workers endeavor, would be essential to achieving the desired endpoint.

Evidence gleaned from other institutions strongly suggested that a controlled, "Small Group Initiative" would be a useful approach to achieving desired results. Small groups, based on group discussions, permit individuals to understand issues (ideas) important to the advancement of the institution, express their opinions regarding those issues, and identify "best practices" regarding application and integration of those ideas into the behavior of the workforce.

An additional Gallup Engagement Survey will be completed by the entire group during July 2019. While more definitive information will be available at that time, observable data already suggest positive results of the Initiative. The decision to continue the Small Group Initiative under direction of Dental School Personnel has been made by the School's leadership.

In the event you are interested, following is a typical agenda:

AGENDA
SMALL GROUP DISCUSSIONS
Session 2
23 July 2018

Each attendee has 2 minutes to introduce the subject and asks each of the remaining attendees to take 2 minutes to comment.

I. Review experiences re Action Plan for the period: 25 June–23 July

    A. What has been the result of recognizing good behavior (performance) in others?

II. Do I know you?

    A. Pick a question and share your thoughts with others.

III. Is there someone at work who encourages my development?

    A. Read "The Sixth Element" (pages 77–90) in the Book: *12 The Elements of Great Managing.*

IV. Discuss the value: *Accountability*

    A. The School of Dentistry is committed to being responsible and transparent. To what extent, as individuals, do we take responsibility for our actions and those of others.

V. Discuss Strategic Plan: *Goal 1: Achieve preeminence as an academic leader through excellence and innovation in patient care, public service, and global engagement.*

VI. Develop Action Plan for Coming Four Weeks *(Facilitator)*

    A. Example:

        1. Discuss taking responsibility with others.

        2. Use pennies as reminder.

As mentioned above, participants completed the Gallup Survey during the period July–August 2018, prior to beginning of the Small Group Initiative. At the end of one year, the Survey was repeated (July–August 2019). Results show that there was meaningful improvement on nine of the twelve parameters[115], a decline on one parameter and essentially no change in the remaining two. There was also notable improvement in a "thirteenth" parameter, which had to do with overall satisfaction of the School as a place to work. Based on these results, Leadership in the Dental School deemed the Small Group Initiative a success and now are in year two of the experiment. It is anticipated there will be an overall improvement in the School's Culture over time. If you have any questions about the small discussion group process, please do not hesitate to reach out to me by email (halchappelear@gmail.com).

---

115. The twelve parameters are 1. Do you know what is expected of you at work? 2. Do you have the materials and equipment to do your work right? 3. At work, do you have the opportunity to do what you do best every day? 4. In the last seven days, have you received recognition or praise for doing good work? 5. Does your supervisor, or someone at work, seem to care about you as a person? 6. Is there someone at work who encourages your development? 7. At work do your opinions seem to count? 8. Does the mission/purpose of your company make you feel your job is important? 9. Are your associates (fellow employees) committed to doing quality work? 10. Do you have a best friend at work? 11. In the last six months, has someone at work talked to you about your progress? 12. In the last year, have you had opportunities to learn and grow?

Harold E. (Hal) Chappelear, LLD (Hon.)

Hal Chappelear is a native of Greenville, South Carolina. He holds a Bachelor of Science in Pharmacy from the Medical University of South Carolina's School, Charleston, South Carolina) and a Doctor of Laws *(honoris causa)* from the University of Maryland, Baltimore, Maryland. Additionally, he completed postgraduate work in psychology and economics at Jacksonville University and the University of Florida.

After participating in the private practice of pharmacy at Community Drug Store and St. Francis Hospital in Greenville, South Carolina, Hal joined The Upjohn Company [Now Pfizer Inc. (NYSC: PFE)] as a sales representative in Anderson, South Carolina, in 1962. He became a member of the company's management ranks in 1967 and, throughout the years that followed, held numerous positions, which included responsibility for North American Operations, Worldwide Marketing Support, and External Affairs. He was a member of the Corporate Management Office, a group of eleven officers responsible for directing the business of The Upjohn Company. He retired from Upjohn September 1, 1992, as a Corporate Executive Vice President.

In October of 1992, Hal joined Medicis Pharmaceutical Corporation [Now Valeant Pharmaceuticals International, Inc. (NYSE: VRX)] currently based in Bridgewater, New Jersey. He served Medicis as President, Chief Operating Officer, and member of the Board of Directors until June 1995. In April 1993, he was appointed Affiliate Professor in the School of Pharmacy at the University of Maryland, Baltimore.

Hal is now a Principal of InternaSource LLC (www.internsource.com) and Member of the Board for Gregory Pharmaceuticals Holdings (GPH), Bristol Tennessee. GPH is a private Company owned by the Gregory family (major stockholders), the University of Maryland, Baltimore, Hal Chappelear, and other minor investors. One of GPH's holdings is UPM Pharmaceuticals (www.upm-inc.com), an independent contract research, development, and manufacturing organization (CDMO) serving the pharmaceutical and biotechnology industries. Following his leadership with support of Dean Knapp and others in the School, UPM had its beginning in The University of Maryland's School of Pharmacy.

As a Principal of InternaSource LLC, he is a private consultant for small businesses, religious, non-profit, and academic institutions. In this capacity, he is engaged in General Business Management, Strategic Planning, Humble Leadership Development, Personal Counseling, and Executive Coaching. He is (or has been) affiliated with South River Restoration, Cell Works (Cancer Research), Dyad Pharmaceuticals (Biotech), University of Maryland, Baltimore (School of Pharmacy, School of Medicine and School of Dentistry), Medical University of South Carolina (School of Pharmacy, School of Dentistry and Foundation for Research Development), and American Society of Health-System Pharmacists.

Hal Chappelear serves on the Board of Trustees of the University of Maryland Baltimore Foundation, Inc., Board of Directors, University of Maryland Baltimore Health Sciences Research Park Corporation, Board of Visitors of the School of Pharmacy, University of Maryland Baltimore, School of Pharmacy, Medical University of South Carolina and Advisor to President and CEO of the Severn Leadership Group (https://www.severnleadership.net/). He has served on the Advisory Boards of the University of Georgia, University of Nebraska, University of Florida, and University of Arizona, Board of Directors of the Severn Leadership Group, Foundation for Critical Care Medicine, the Kalamazoo Symphony Society, the Research and Education Foundation of the American Society of Health-System Pharmacists (ASHP) and the Health Sciences Foundation of the Medical University of South Carolina.

On July 17, 2002, the United States Coast Guard Licensed Dr. Chappelear as a U. S. Merchant Marine Officer.

On March 29, 2006, Hal was inducted into the Beta Chi chapter of Phi Lambda Sigma at the Medical University of South Carolina. Phi Lambda Sigma is an honor society focused on Pharmacy Leadership.

His biographical sketch has been published in Marquis Who's Who in America and Who's Who in Finance and Industry.

Hal Chappelear and his wife Billie currently reside in Annapolis, Maryland. They have two children: Alan Todd (deceased) and Amy Elizabeth of Millersville, Maryland.